CU00869218

Gouri Sadotra

The Beautiful People Club

A fictional first novel

by Gouri Sadotra

Dedication

I would like to dedicate this first book of mine
to my mother and father for all of their love
and support over the years.
First published in 2015

ISBN :

Text and footnotes registered copyright ©
Gouri Sadotra 7th December 2015

Typeset in Great Britain by Gouri Sadotra
2015

The Beautiful People Club

Contents

The Beautiful People Club

Chapter 1

Alex as usual was watching the Beautiful People, silently observing their common characteristics and noting it down in his head for further analysis at a later date. It was the perfect pass time, something everyone did consciously or unconsciously. A woman had just walked by. Let the game begin, thought Alex.

She was in her mid-forties, it was obvious through the subtle engravings of age etched on her face. Alex found her beautiful. Extrapolating her every gesture he examined her psyche based on the scant pieces of information that her gestures suggested.

He was bog eyed with fascination at the posh lady's pop-eyed expression of feigned interest at her companion's (obviously) scintillating conversation. The lady was seated at the center table of a fashionable eatery in the most fashionable part of town. This was the restaurant of choice for the rich and beautiful, a place to observe and a place to be observed.

Her minute movements were magnified by her sheer emphasis on the manner of proper decorum necessary to eat a chicken sandwich. Every two minutes her right hand would delicately daub her painted lips with a paper napkin. Legs crossed, back straight, eating unnaturally slowly as if the sheer act of digestion was beneath her. Did she live on air alone? That was the obvious conclusion that Alex drew.

Smiling politely at the waiter who cleared her table, as if she really was not a discriminating person! It was all a front. Observing everyone and everything whilst appearing to look only at her seated guest she epitomized the expression "eyes at the back of your head".

Watching me, watching you thought Alex. We all watch each other.

And so our story begins….

The Beautiful People Club

Chapter 2

It was a humid day in the offices of the accountant's firm Jonathon C. Cameron and Associates, although this in itself was not unusual for London in July. The sun was shining outside and all around London people were scurrying from one place to another to get away from the abominable heat wave that had submerged London into one of the worst droughts it had seen in over one hundred years.

Inside the office of Jonathon C. Cameron, Max sat on her chair fidgeting wildly. It was an interior designer's dream room. The soft leather sofas in the lobby beckoned with the promise to hold you in the most upright position and the walls painted with muted colours of beige and the occasional red brick wall design peeping through, showing expertly laid bricks of a master bricklayer. The miniature trees were real and the soil in the pots contained wood shavings for a more artistic or was it more uniform design function. Had the accountancy profession become so sophisticated? And if so when? All of this was light years from the small wall paper peeling office that her father had sat in. Even the receptionist, who alluded to her more stylish title of front office assistant, was artfully designated to a desk that met her every need and yet performed the requisite amount of style sensationalism that Max had come to expect from the accountancy firm of Jonathon C. Cameron.

Despite the fans that were buzzing around the office, the warm humid air surrounded Max like an invisible cloud and beads of perspiration trickled down to the small of her back soaking her shirt which lay tucked beneath her very proper navy blue jacket with its gold anchor motif buttons. She was uncomfortable.

Next to her sat James. James, another trainee, was working diligently as usual. He seemed to be impervious to the heat, fans and noise of the city streets below as he turned page after page of crisp A4 paper that lay on his desk. People hardly moved in this office to talk or make coffee or even go to the toilet. Only when they couldn't stand it any more did they succumb. In the office protocol demanded a professional appearance and coupled with that a professional demeanor, which in turn meant not socializing during work hours. Of course no one ever said anything, it was merely understood by the manner in which the senior staff in the firm behaved. The trainees took note and followed suit guarding their professional standing with great care.

Every year the firm hired twenty or so trainees on placements. They would be taught in all four areas of accountancy and at the end of each course would receive examinations. At the end of the their placements the best and the brightest of those who passed their examinations would be offered jobs with a view to a partnership by their late twenties or early thirties.

This was not to say that there was never any fun in the office. But it was minimal. Joke emails were sent to trainees by trainees and to trusted senior staff. The previous year the office server went down, as the intranet had been flooded with so many none-work related emails sent by bored trainees to one another. Eventually they had called a staff meeting and everyone was warned that the number of emails would be monitored and they hoped that the number of non-work related emails would go down. This had not stopped the trainees they still sent emails to one another but Max did not participate in that. She only sent work-related emails to James, which infuriated him as she sat in the desk next to him. Why couldn't she be human for once and just ask him instead of just sending him an email. Or perhaps it was pride, perhaps she was just too proud to admit that she ever needed help from him.

James had been a trainee for over seventeen months and by his record was touted to becoming a partner one day. First he would have to pass his final round of accountancy examinations in November, later that year. He turned to ask Max a question; after all he was her mentor and was responsible for her well being in the office. 'Max, When will we have lunch again?' He had left the question open but not too open he wanted the meaning to be clear, determination without the gentle hint of desperation. She smiled mysteriously and said that she was busy today. He was internally furious. That was his line, he was her superior and yet she had succeeded in making him subservient to her faintest whims and wishes.

She was busy, she was busy she was always busy. Why was she always busy? Even for the conservative office of Jonathon C. Cameron she was extraordinarily diligent. Perhaps she had her eye on a partnership. Yes that could be it thought James, but then again perhaps she doesn't like me. Then who did she like in the office? She was an escape artiste nonpareil. Always avoiding staff, she ate her meals on her own he suspected and despite various attempts by some of the other female trainees she rebuffed their attempts at friendship just as she all rebuffed all male attempts at dates, making her the most unpopular trainee in the office. She was so mysterious and so strange he thought as if she belonged to no one and her life began and ended in the office. Why was she so strange? Why doesn't she make an attempt to fit in he pondered. He would never have given her behaviour a second thought had she not been Max.

Max, the strange girl with the large luminous black eyes! She was Indian but not apparently so. She had pale creamy skin that James longed to touch. Not quite as vampirishly white as she would have hoped but pale enough to cause a startling contrast to her mane of black wavy hair and her almost red lips, red, as they were smeared with a poppy red lipstick today, as always. He could only imagine what the colour of her naked lips would look like. Her lips, that he had studied when he felt that she was not looking, were curved into a magnificent pout especially when she was sad. She was beautiful, the most beautiful woman that he had ever met. Yet she had the saddest eyes that he had ever seen.

Tentatively he decided to talk to her again, after all he had a break coming up as he had been working diligently all morning and she was worth it. 'What are you doing?' Without raising her head from the desk she replied that she was working. 'No, at lunch time, what are you doing then?' 'I've got things to do, nothing really exciting really, just stuff.' Now it was his turn to smile as he scanned the room seeing if anyone was watching his behaviour. "Gotcha" he thought to himself, "I'm gonna pin you down for sure this time". 'What kind of stuff?' Then she muttered about phoning a friend. Why did she do that? Why did she always do that? She drove him crazy. She never called her 'friends' by their names; instead she turned the noun, friend, into a proper noun. Did she have hundreds of friends or just one, he did not know. He had never seen her being friendly with anyone and at the summer barbeque two weeks ago she had arrived and left alone. He had been sitting next to her for three months and still he knew only the merest hint of details from her life. Max did not even have the courtesy to be interested in his life.

This time, he decided that he was going to unravel the mystery. He felt brave enough to ask the question that he had never asked before. He swiveled his chair around so that he was facing her. Now he was poised for attack. 'So which friend are you phoning today?' Max turned to face him he noticed that her eyes had suddenly become fierce. 'My best friend' she said sarcastically. Her answer was forbidding or was it? He had ventured into unchartered territory. So far no one in the office had managed to make Max admit that she loved or cared for anything.

'Your best friend, does she have a name?' Yes he does replied Max. James laughed to himself so this was it her secret boyfriend. He already knew that she was Indian and had often suspected and hoped that she had a wild side to her character but he had never believed her to be a closeted Indian female whose parents did not allow her a boyfriend, perhaps he was wrong and she just was not allowed out of the house. Either that or she has a married lover and she is having an illicit affair with him. That would explain it. Her secretive behaviour, the silent sulks that lasted for days and all the while he could feel that there were hot rages inside her just waiting to erupt like a volcano. I am going to dissect you he thought. 'What is his name?' he asked nonchalantly. 'His name' she spat out, 'Is none of your business'.

'Why so secretive Max, don't you trust me?' She said with full confidence, after regaining her composure to his taunt 'It is my experience not to trust anybody until I know them very well.' The sting in her remark caught her in his face. He went red and then felt angry. There was no need to be angry really, after all he was a cool guy, a cooool guy, too cool to be destabilized by her jibe.

'I trusted my friends.'

'I see' he mused. Internally he was confused what did she mean? She was talking in the past tense. Did that mean that she trusted nobody since the beginning? Or that her boyfriend had deceived her and since then she trusted no one? No wonder Max is so secretive, so sly. His eyes glistened triumphantly at his discovery but at the same time he was racked with jealousy and a desire to find out more.

He would try another line of attack. 'Max if you ever need anyone to talk to I hope you feel that you can come to talk to me as not only am I your mentor but I hope your friend too. It's just that it has been noted that you don't socialize with the rest of the staff. I am not trying to worry you and it is not as if your hard work has not been appreciated but we at Jonathon C. Cameron like to keep a friendly atmosphere and your attitude is being seen as a bit of a hindrance.' You're a sneaky snake thought James. Actually none of his superiors had told him to tell him that infact they had all commended him on doing a good job on the new trainee who was no bother at all. Of course James insisted that the monthly mentor lunches were necessary to make sure that she stayed on track remaining an asset to Jonathon C. Cameron.

Max had not mentioned it but the reason why she had chosen this firm was its size and its dedication to hard work. The rewards were high but the price that you had to pay was loyalty to the job. So when James told her that her silence had been noted she knew that he was lying. No one was going to criticise her for not socializing within the office hours. She said nothing but merely wore an expression of incredulity. James caught Max's eye at that very moment; he understood exactly what she had been thinking. He was stumped, what should he do, why did he lie to her of all people when it was most important for him to be open, honest and approachable to her.

Finally Max replied, 'It's not that I don't trust you, its just that I don't know you. I know that I can be perceived to be aloof but I like to keep my personal life separate from my office life so that I can concentrate more on my work.' Despite her avoiding to answer his question he was aware of the truth in her statement, he and many of the more successful trainees did the same, keeping their private lives private so that there would be no trouble for them at work and in their career any hint of a troubled private life could lead to repercussions in the respective career. James immediately understood the conundrum before him, in order for her to trust him she needed to feel secure with him, but before she could feel secure with him she had to trust him. Catch 22, but isn't it always the way with beautiful girls. They always drove you crazy in one way or another.

'Listen Max, I don't mean to pry but if you really want someone to talk to then I hope you know that you can talk to me.' He had attempted one last stab at making her his own. 'It's not that I don't want to talk to you its just that we are starting to attract attention.' She was right. James turned around and noticed one of the partners talking to a secretary, he could have been asking her to do some typing for him or he could have been asking how long James and Max had been taking to each other. James had just had an attack of paranoia. 'Well when and where do you want to talk?' Despite his paranoia he maintained his cool, after all he could just be talking to his pupil helping her out with some work that she was troubled with. With that thought, he lifted a piece of paper and started pointing at it and nodding. Then he turned to Max and said 'Pretend that you are working. I think that Jenkins has noticed us talking.' 'How about we meet at the Taj Mahal restaurant after work at eight? It is Friday after all and this is going to take some time I suppose.' Said Max. James was flushed with the first round of victory and he agreed.

With that James swung around back to his desk and began to analyse the conversation that he had just had with Max. What would she tell him? He began to get worried that her dark secrets may in fact be commonplace and mundane. That her boyfriend, the worthless creep, was with another woman, or that he was married, or he was cheating on her. He hated her imaginary boyfriend and hoped that Max hated him too. He looked at his watch it was five thirty. It was an expensive RADA watch that he had treated to himself on getting this job. He had saved the money and brought it for himself in the January sales. One day it will be a Rolex, when I make partner.

At eight O'clock. James turned to look at Max, she was rising from a desk and then she started to shuffle her papers into position for the next day. He also rose and collected his red leather briefcase from under the nest of draws under his desk. He straightened his jacket and tie before addressing Max, 'Are you ready?' She said yes. They then walked the long walk towards the elevators. They met several other trainees and James nodded authoritatively towards them. Max merely ignored them and continued to march. There was a look of surprise and slight awe that someone had managed to get a date with Max and that 'we are all boys together' smug look that men give to one another. They waited at the elevator for the elevator to arrive after the big mahogany doors leading away from the office had closed they were joined by Jenkins the partner that had earlier that day seen them talking together. James pushed his weight from one foot to another in an effort to calm his nerves. Attractive as Max was James was anxious to avoid the rumour that they were having an office romance, but Max was unperturbed. There was silence in the elevator and the doors opened and shut letting in more people from different floors who were also anxious to leave the building. Finally they reached ground floor and Max and James left but not before James had said goodbye to Jenkins.

The air outside was moist and the sun was beginning to fall in the sky although you could still see it. It was still quite hot and the crowds on the streets were more subdued as they were enjoying the early evening night air as they rushed past walking, jumping into taxis or catching buses. James instinctively reached out for Max's hand 'I don't want to loose you in the rush' he said justifying his action half to himself. Max merely deigned to have her hand held. After a five minute walk they reached the restaurant, which was already filled with people. The Indian restaurant was coloured in reds, black and burgundies and the lights had already been dimmed and the candles in the hurricane lamps were lit. There were sounds of Bollywood songs being played in the background. They were all set for an intimate dinner for two.

They waited in the lobby for the waiter to give them a table. As they walked to the table Max loosened her hand from his grip 'I won't get lost in the rush to the dinner table James.' They ordered drinks and snacks from the bar. Max then said, I am sorry for dragging you out like this its just that I want to have some one to talk to but I think I have forgotten how to confide in anyone. I've kept my own counsel for what seems like such a long time that I don't know how to talk to anyone without overwhelming them.'

James gave his best 'You can trust me look' and it was enough.

'Well' said Max frowning slightly as tiny furrow formed in her forehead. I am not sure how to begin. It's really complex and such a long story I only hope that we have the time.' James said that he had all the time in the world, it was Friday night and he had nothing planned for the rest of the night.

The Beautiful People Club

Chapter 3

I am not saying that it's good; I am not saying that it's right. I am just saying that this is the way that it really happened.

I was a first year in a small old university with a long established history and was keen to experience all the delights of university life. Unlike other students who had boyfriends and girlfriends at home or at other universities I had no one waiting for me. The first week, Fresher's week, was dedicated to having fun and making friends before lectures started. Wanting to enjoy myself to the fullest, I planned on going to every party, every club and every pub each night. Every night I was with my flat mates we went out together as we were all first years and had not made our friends.

I still remember my first drink. It had been vodka and orange. I had ordered it from the bar on the first night out when I was with my flat mates. Although only eighteen years old most of them were already habitual drinkers and I was embarrassed to admit to them that I had never drunk or been drunk until that very moment. The taste of the vodka and orange reminded me of rotten oranges that were losing their sweetness and had taken on an alcoholic taste. I was not impressed but I was nervous so I kept sipping. Very soon I had drunk the entire drink and it had left a dry taste in my mouth. I could feel myself exhaling alcohol in my breath as I breathed through my mouth. I was about to order another drink when a flat mate asked if I was very rich. I said no and they told me that vodka was expensive and I should drink beer instead. So I tried beer. It was revolting but I drank it anyway. To this day I have never liked beer and since then stuck to spirits. By this time I was merry and I kept on drinking all night only to be literally carried home by my flat mates. I woke the next morning with my first hangover, which oddly enough I cherished as a sign of my emerging adulthood. From that day on I was a drinker.

Later that week my flat mates and I decided to go to a club where the university band would be playing. It sounded like a good idea, as we were sick of all of the drinking that was compulsory in our university. Over the past week I had made friends with a foreign exchange student and we exchanged addresses his name was Tomas and was French. He looked like a visiting lecturer and was treated with respect, by both students and faculty alike, that was not awarded to Fresher's like myself. This was mainly because he dressed in the way that most first years imagine their lecturers would look like. He agreed to meet me that night at the pub and from there we would go to the club where we would meet my flat mates.

Tomas was tall, handsome and very affectionate. He would pull me closer to him as we sat on the bar stools of the university bar whilst he drank beer. He had dark brown hair and the warmest brown eyes and was tanned all over from spending the summer on the beach in Spain working as a bartender. I was infatuated with him. It was premature, still but I had started planning my life around him already as I was hoping to spend time with him until he left to go back to his home in France at the end of the year.

We had never discussed his leaving but I had no doubt that he would meet someone else when he was back in France again so I only planned to maintain the relationship while he was in England with me. I was pragmatic about my romantic liaisons. I had always believed that I was able to control my feelings over anyone so that I would never get too closely attached to anyone. Why did I feel this way? It was in part my fears of failure, I had never failed academically in anything and partly because never wanted anyone to control me via my feelings towards them, but also it was fear of falling in love. Not that I believed in love, well not for me, but I wanted to fall in love at the right time but when it was convenient, when I didn't have study pressures or pressure from my parents telling me to succeed. I was the eldest child in my family and the first to go to university and I did not want to let down the family that was so proud of me.

Tomas suited me. I suited him neither of us was looking for a long-term commitment only temporary happiness while it lasted with one another. Both of us had our goals that we did not want to shirk from. After we met at the bar we had a few drinks and then we went to the club. It was eleven thirty already and the streets were filled with students and locals alike all drunk and looking for a good night out. We queued to get into the club and the smoke from Tomas's Gauloise cigarettes clung to my clothes as we hugged each other for a bit of extra warmth. My hands were in his jacket pockets, while he embraced me and covered my face with smoke scented kisses.

When we got into the club the bands session had ended and the club was overflowing with students drunk on beer and spirits. We also went to the bar to get more drinks and enjoy our last weekend until our lectures started. The crowd to the bar was stifling and Tomas and I were separated as we made our way to the bar. A hand grabbed my waist, now I was beginning to get used to this, as this was 'Fuck A Fresher' week. I turned my face up to look at him. That moment I met Alexander Thomas. 'But you can call me Alex' he said. He had only a passing acquaintance with reality; they had parted company along time ago. Alex epitomized a chic that most people could only aspire to. He looked like a lion; his hair fell in corkscrew curls like a golden waterfall down his back and his brown eyes moved languidly as he observed everything with hawk-like detachment.

He was smiling at me so I smiled back to him and then he smiled again. I turned to move away to get back to Tomas who was now observing us enraged whilst he was holding our drinks. I turned to walk towards Tomas as Alex was pulling me closer to him. 'Why are you running away?' he said. I'm not running away I retorted. He'd already entranced me but he was drunk and I did not want to be the easy lay of a drunken second or third year so I decided to leave him and return to Tomas. Tomas asked me who I was talking to I could tell that he was already jealous as he suspected that there had been a spark between Alex and myself. To allay his fears I merely told him that it was nobody I knew. Which was the truth. We returned to the small dance floor and began dancing together while he continued to smoke his French cigarettes. All the while I could see Alex watching me as we danced as Ed the DJ played the summer hits of that year. Alex didn't look angry merely surprised. He was with a group of his friends who were laughing and cheering around him. That, I thought, would be the end of it.

That night Tomas and I talked as we walked back from the club past the promenade to our halls of residence. It was a starry night of the deepest dark blue backdrop against the angry black waves of the sea that crashed past us as we walked. He told me about his life in France when he had been a student. The French university system allows everyone an opportunity to further education. That right is enshrined in their constitution. Yet there were problems. They have huge lecture theatres seating thousands of students and it is hard to hear and study. Every year there are examinations and if you fail you are kicked out of university. As you can imagine each year the lecture theatres get emptier and emptier. Tomas barely made it through university but he was very intelligent, I could tell. He was studying for his Masters over here and was using this as a way of proving to himself that he was capable of hard work and academic accomplishment. 'I'm a stupid' he used to say humorously 'because I have the capability and instead I wasted my time drinking, smoking and chasing women.' His English was very good and his French accent was slight and sexy.

That weekend I had reserved for sobering up. I had drunk an almighty amount of alcohol and I could still feel it pulsating in my veins the next morning when the alarm rang I slammed it down and continued sleeping. When I woke again it was past midday and my head was still spinning out of control. I reached for a glass of water to calm down the dull pulsating rhythm that had taken over my brain waves. I had a shower washing away the previous night from my hair and from my skin. I got dressed in a clean-ish pair of blue jeans a t-shirt and a jumper. I hated wearing shirts as did not like ironing them. All my other clothes smelled of cigarette smoke, I didn't smoke myself but spending time with Tomas had made my clothes reek of old, stale, musty cigarettes. The smell from my clothes made the air in my bedroom smell too, so I opened the small narrow window to let in some fresh and rather cold air and a cold blast caught me unaware.

It was time to do the laundry. I had plenty of practice doing the laundry as a child unlike some of the students in university who I later learned had their mothers doing their laundry in the weekends. I gathered all of my clothes in a big black plastic bag and slung it over my shoulder holding the washing powder in my other hand I proceeded to find my way to the laundry room situated underneath our halls of residence. Finding an empty washing machine I dumped the contents of my dirty clothes into the washing machine, mixing both whites and colors. I had learnt that if you washed on a medium heat colorfast clothes the colors don't run, fade, but do get clean. My own personal previous experience of washing machines was that they never washed white clothes white unless they were pretty clean to begin with. I turned to leave when I bumped into someone. We both apologized simultaneously. It turned out that her name was Katie and she was a Fresher too. She was smoking a cigarette and it was dangling from her mouth as she dragged washed wet clothes from the washing machine into the drier. We decided to meet for a coffee in the Student's Union. On such flimsy basis friendships were made in the first week. Yes that's how I met Katie.

Katie had succeeded in circumventing the history of her genes and was five foot ten tall. She was by definition "lines", a hardbody, sinew and muscle, angular and taut. Katie was a beach-blonde, bleach-blonde with a glacial demeanour and eyebrows plucked to oblivion. Very eye catching don't you think? She had already secured a job in the Student's Union working behind the bar on weekends and she proceeded to tell me of all of her sexual exploits that week over a steaming cappuccino.

She had been at the club the night Alex was talking to me. She had already made his acquaintance the night before and had had sex with him. He was very good in bed she confided. They had had sex twice that night. It had been her first time…or so she insisted. She amazed me at the openness at which she discussed her newfound sex life. She was part of the sexually active population. Between close friends this type of talk was understandable but between strangers? This was another thing I had to learn about university life I had never wanted that to 'lose it' on a first night stand, that much of my Indian culture I had retained within me. My virginity was not something I particularly cherished, nor was it something I was anxious to loose. I was curious about sex especially as things were becoming more sexual between Tomas and I. But I was not ready. Katie made me feel sexually inarticulate.

She was already planning her impending relationship with Alex and the fact that he had made a move on me had not deterred her in the slightest. He would be her future husband and the father of her children she said gushingly to me. I merely gulped down my cappuccino. Last night she had been waiting for him to approach her but he had not he had merely said hello to her and from that she had hoped that he would come back to her again but he had then met me.

Well I could see why she was attracted to Alex he was certainly very handsome; no that's not the word. His hair and face were beautiful in a way that women are described. He possessed a beguilingly feminine beauty encompassed by his girlie glamourous hair. His face was composed of small regular features of almost female proportions that when taken separately were not extraordinary but all together the effect was astonishing without being effeminate. He was a masculine man in his behaviour. Strong and athletically built although only five foot ten he was the picture of beauty in motion. And the way he dressed. He wore only the most fashionable clothes that covered his body alluringly in his fitted trousers that hugged his narrow waist and his tight tops that showed off his tanned muscular arms. He was tanned even though he was a blond Englishman in September, in Britain let me add.

I in turn told her about Tomas and how we met each other. I was in our faculty department trying to find out where I had to register on the first day that I arrived. I turned to a young man who I thought was a lecturer to ask him but he said he was looking for the same department to register himself. Then we met again outside the phone booths of our student halls of residence. We had both reached for the phone at the same time and our hands had touched. Then we both asked the other one to go first eventually I went first and phoned my parents and he took the phone next to me, which had just been vacated. The next time I saw him was in the coffee shop outside the Student's Union and he came over to talk to me he said he liked me and would I have coffee with him, actually I had coffee and a few kisses later that day in his dorm. After that we would meet two three times a day. I would walk down to his halls of residence taking a chance that he would be in and he would do the same. We met frequently under the "serendipity principle". We never organized our meetings, we met spontaneously, and hence it was a happy accident when we bumped into each other.

After my chat with Katie I left the Students Union coffee bar, passing small shopkeepers on stalls that had been installed in the hallway of the Union. They were selling silk scarves, Indian batik sheets, bedspreads and all manner of incense and aromatherapy oils and burners. Another vendor was selling posters of pictures by Dali, Van Gogh and the Impressionists. I brought nothing for my bare student room and instead hurried back to the launderette to collect my washed clothes and put them in the drier. After drying them I went back to my dorm. It was already mid afternoon and I was starting to feel better, more sober. I had astonished myself when I started drinking in university as no one in my family had ever touched a drop, and they would be angry and disappointed to know that I had started but in the immortal words of Oscar Wilde, 'I had no desire to undeceive them'. I let them think through my phone calls that I was still their little girl. Behind this change in my behavior lay a desire. I wanted to transcend my Indian Background. Some people want to be someone else, but I wanted to be myself but different, better, and by doing these things I would be better. University, unlike real life, is the place where you could be exactly what you wanted to be.

On Monday morning the first year students in my faculty were scheduled to have a meeting with the Dean of the department. I had overslept and missed this meeting arriving fifteen minutes late and I was too nervous to enter the lecture theatre for fear of being labeled 'the tardy one' for the rest of the three years. I waited outside for students to emerge so that I could grab one of them and ask what had happened. After waiting forty minutes I gleaned that we were to attend lectures and tutorials each week both were compulsory and on top of that we had assignments to do in preparation for the tutorials and lastly we had to submit essays which were to be completed on time and handed in to the subject tutors pigeon hole. In the middle of the second semester and the end of the third semester we would have examinations and the pass mark was forty percent. If we failed all our subjects we would be ejected from this university. I then rushed to the lecture theatre to collect the handouts that the other students had received from the Dean. I later heard that the Dean was a fat, overbearing bully – well first impressions can be very persuasive although I personally had not had a chance to assess him.

I then had a small group meeting with my tutor. All the first years had been put in tutorial groups under the guidance of a lecturer to whom we were informed would be there to give us guidance, of what kind was not specified. My tutor was a fine lady who unfortunately had a minor speech impediment. She stuttered. I only presumed that years of teaching had enabled her to overcome most of it. As a group in a meeting we all sat deep into our black plastic chairs. I looked at my hands placed in my lap. No one uttered a single word despite Ms. Braithwaite's forced attempts at joviality. Instead I looked at the walls, the backs of the photograph frames on her desk and her unfortunate taste in animal print jumpers, in fact anything but look at her. I was intimidated talking to her. It was a new sensation. At school I had been a champion talker and had often been told to be quiet so that other students could have a chance to have their say, but here and now when it counted the most I was unable to mutter an intelligible word except to say my name, surname and the town I came from.

I longed to be able to hold intelligent discourses with my lecturers and my peers dazzling them with my wit and sheer brilliance but I was unable to do so. I was in the shadows. Later over coffee in the Student's Union, I told all of this to Tomas. He merely smiled and told me not to be so keen to prove myself. 'You are something very special Max and I do like you for it. You are vigorous and full of creative energy and this motivates me'. I smiled and leaned over. I could smell the scent of coffee mixed with tobacco as we kissed each other. It was not an altogether unpleasant taste.

I turned around and there was Katie, looking like an extra from Blade Runner in her black leather pants, she walked up to us. She was holding a flier in her hands. "Hey how are you?" whilst speaking to me she was looking at Tomas. She was desperate for an introduction, I could tell. Maintaining his mystique, Tomas reached for another cigarette, she turned to him and asked for a drag. I was surprised at the intimacy of the request. He merely offered a Galuoise to her and then to me. We both accepted. Not wanting to be left out of this smoking coterie I put the cigarette to my lips and lit it. I did not know what to do, my brain was working furiously, should I inhale or exhale to light the cigarette? Rapidly I did both. Tomas and Katie were in tears of laughter as they saw me cough up the contents of my lungs after a single exhalation. Yes this was my first cigarette. I continued to smoke that cigarette under the joint pupilage of Katie and Tomas.

The flier beckoned with its bright blue paper. We proceeded to read it. Inside were the usual greetings welcoming both current and new students to the University. There were try-outs for all the usual sports teams, hockey, football, rugby and swimming. Also was an advertisement for the Student magazine. They wanted poems, short stories of student experiences at university in fact anything you cared to write about. I glanced over everything, not paying real attention until Katie pointed out a notice that the student gym had been refurbished and the machines upgraded. This meant nothing to Tomas and myself, neither were gym fanatics. Katie on the other hand, despite her dedication to cigarettes and alcohol was already a member of the student gym, working out three to four times a week in order to maintain her model like physique. At the bottom of the page was a poem by an unknown student author. It was called Space-Time Continuum.

I feel sad at all the things I could have done that day but didn't
All the moments that flew by
And all I ever really wanted to do was to find a hole in the space-time continuum.
Where I could pause, and imagine and absorb everything going around me
See all the sights, because there really never is enough time to do everything

And even if I live to be one million years old
I never will read every book
Understand every subtle nuance
Hear every sound of music
Observe the heavenly bodies realign whilst they twinkle through a gossamer cloud

Or view the tremble of a leaf at any given
autumnal day
See what life is like at any given moment

I wonder how I would press the pause button on
my life
Would everybody stand still, like Grecian statutes
Would the wind cease?
Or would there be a continual stream of air?
Would my hair be suspended by a single gust of
wind?

A hole in the space-time continuum
Where life pauses but you can walk around
The moment your life ceases

I sympathized with the secret sorrow of the
author who did reveal his or her name. What
tragedy made him or her feel like this when all
around there were seemingly happy people? A
moment later the poem and its effect was
forgotten as the three of us all had more pressing
problems of life, courses and how to tackle.

Officially lectures started on Wednesday. There
was still time to mess around with Tomas before
the real work began. In all things academic, I felt
that I was the archetypal nerd, always craving
attention for my compositions. Wanting love,
approval, everything. Wanting the world, all the
while thinking how to achieve my goals. I was
prepared for everything. Or so I thought.

The Beautiful People Club

Chapter 4

Rushing to the lecture hall to arrive on time for the first lecture on European History I was late. By five minutes. Walking in alone and embarrassed, the students turned to stare. Stupidly I had walked in at the front. Making a mental note in my head I decided that in future, if late again, to walk through the back entrance so that no one would see me or be disturbed. This was an exercise in embarrassment management.

The lecturer, John Cartwright, droned on. His words were a buzz in my fuzzy head. Still suffering from the previous night's drinking session, I soldiered on. Diligently making notes of the important issues in Bismarck's domestic policies. Fifty minutes later it was over. Thank the Lord.

Time for a cigarette break.

In the two days since my first cigarette I had been practicing smoking. Firstly the technical side, how to smoke without spluttering. After ten attempts I mastered that phase of the program. Later came the artistic side, how to smoke stylishly. I had noted that some smokers, usually hardened smokers, wolfed down their cigarette in a race to smoke as quickly as possible. This was done by inhaling deeply into the cigarette and drawing all of the smoke into the lungs and then exhaling out a plume of smoke. Others, such as Katie and Tomas smoked elegantly, in a carefree manner, for them smoking was a pleasure to be savored. It was the latter group that I wanted to emulate.

This was the first cigarette of the morning. Already I had nearly finished my first packet of twenty. Like Katie, American cigarettes were the cigarettes of choice for me. I opened the soft-top packet taking out the lighter that was also in the packet. Putting my cigarette to my lips I surveyed my surroundings. Always I had a fear that a relative would emerge from nowhere and see me doing this 'wicked deed'. Max smoking, what will the neighbors say? I was a bad girl now. That thought both tormented me whilst giving satisfaction. Looking around nervously, this was the first time I had smoked outside. It was very nerve racking. What would the other people think of me? No one noticed me huddled against the rain in the corner. Everybody else was doing exactly the same, chatting and smoking. It was the natural thing to do.

Finishing my cigarette, I stubbed it out against the red brick wall and walked away from the crime scene nonchalantly in the wet September air. Crossing the square that lay in the middle of the campus I saw the throngs of students jostling against one another in a rush to get to a particular building. North, South, East, West. In every direction they rushed like small insects their standard uniform, denim. With the rain in my face I walked back to my room.

Opening my second hand history book on Bismarck, I began to read. I was covering old ground. Everything was familiar but just the requisite standard for essay submissions had been pushed up an octave. I was confident of success. Despite all my current actions to the contrary, lay a desire to do well, to do so well as to get a Distinction when I left the University. Later after discussing this topic with my peers I came to realize that this was a common goal amongst all first years. Three years of substance abuse would distort this reality for all but the most doggedly determined students, but I was determined to be amongst that handful.

After I finished the chapter I looked at the lecture hand out. There was the suggested further reading. Collecting pen, paper, files, all the paraphernalia of study, I marched down to the library. I knew the direction from Fresher's week. It was a large ugly 70's building. Set against the gothic architecture of the older buildings, it was unsightly, in fact a downright eyesore. Nevertheless it had its benefits. It was warm, carpeted, well lit, had plenty of space to study and do research and kept the books and archival records from getting damp in the winter. This was a huge improvement on the previous building, which had now found a new calling as a Center for Arts and Culture as well as containing a cafeteria. After it was refurbished in the late 1980's.

In this cafeteria lecturers could be seen lurking drinking cups of tea from proper white china, in an attempt to get away from their bothersome students, of the first year and third year variety. Second years were known to be too busily involved in their extra curricular activities to bother them. First years were known to be desperate for "Lecturer Attention Syndrome", whilst Third years were desperate for help in their dissertations. I flattered myself that I was neither and instead embraced an ice-cold restraint that penetrated my motions. I was officially too cool to care!

I walked into the musty hall of the library. The sound of my footsteps muffled by the once thick carpeting that covered the second floor building. Tube lighting hung from the lowered ceilings and pop art graced the walls. It was the Seventies revisited. It was still early in the day. Students were already congregating around bookshelves trying to find that all important piece of evidence that would piece together their thesis and dissertations. First years? There were none to be seen. Except for the most diligent who had already committed to memory the reading lists and were compiling their notes already in preparation for the bi annual examinations.

I collected my books, photocopied my articles and left the library. Mission accomplished. Now began the arduous task of compiling notes in preparation for the examinations. That I would do in the luxury of my room.

Later that day I emerged, dazed but triumphant, eating the coffee from my cup. I had drank that much. As I turned to open another packet of cigarettes, I noticed the note that had been shoved under my door.

Dear Max,

Darling, I miss you very much. Meet me in the Student's bar for a drink. 8pm sharp. I want to take you out tonight.

Tomas

I smiled. I turned to open the cigarette packet when Katie burst in through my door. I showed her the note and she smiled ruefully. Her pursuit of Alex was not proving successful. Yet she was not disheartened. We discussed male-female battle plans and methods on how to out-maneuver and manipulate men. All in all, it was a fun afternoon's conversation.

With ever decreasing circles of innocence, I walked that long walk alone to the Student's bar. Maybe I was a product of my environment or hereditary cultural terrorism that engrossed young Indian girls (and boys) with a love of all European fashions. I was a prime example of this counter culture, this phenomenon. This cultural war, east verses west this Kulturkampf. My parents had gone so far, now I would go further. I had no great love of Indian culture, religion or society. These were the shackles that held me back from being the kind of person I wanted to be. India was as alien and unfamiliar to me as the Roman Empire was to modern day Italians. Years of mutual self-suppression and parental "guidance" and I had still emerged to be a thoroughly Anglicized Indian girl. I was the archetypical Indian girl, following European fashions. After all, only nerds wore Indian clothes. Yet despite all those years of rejection lay a dormant kernel of pride in being Indian.

Tomas was sitting on a bar stool sipping a long drink while a new student band were ushered onto the stage. The singer, a tall handsome boy with pale blue eyes began to speak. "Hi I'm Nick and this song is dedicated to all those ladies out there that are a little salty, that are a little sweet. The song is called "the first taste of you"

The first taste of you, you devoured me

It was all of you
And how you showered me
With love and kisses and what not things
And how I felt,
It was meant to be and everything

The first kiss of you, inspired me
To have your lips around fired me
With thoughts and desires and dreams of
momentous things
How I felt, how you are, about everything

The first bite of you, how it lightened me
It was all of you inside of me
With love, a weightless thing and dreams of you
forever real
I keep beside me, with all my zeal

The first taste of you, both tart and sweet
Exhilaration it gave me heat
That smooth skin, the tender heart
You made me quiver, you made me shake
You drove your love through my heart like a
stake

Know that it was the first taste of you
That started it all

Nick had a speaking voice to match his singing
voice; with rounded vowels it was articulate and
smooth. The intonation was perfect. Most singers
destroy the illusion they have created when they

begin to speak, but not so Nick. Whilst he sang he imitated a faux-American accent and style, but when he spoke it was with the crystal clear accent of Southern England. It was pure Hugh Grant in voice only, not mannerisms. There was no invention so to speak; he merely verbalized reality.

You couldn't just help but stare at him as he walked in that cool walk. He walked the walk. Soon he would talk the talk and he would be unstoppable. Those in the crowd cheered uproariously, for he had a truly melodious voice and a face and physique to match. He was one of life's winners. And nobody envied his success they merely wanted to join in his celebrations, his success.

I turned to Tomas and planted a long lingering kiss on his neck. I was feeling brave and sexy. Years of sexual suppression oozed out like honey. He turned to face me barely able to stand up. He was already drunk. He had been drinking since the bar opened. I was not shocked but was disappointed. This was not turning out to be the night I had imagined it to be.

The band began their next song as I heaved Tomas's weight onto me. I could barely walk up the winding narrow path that led to the Student Village, where Tomas lived. It was set high up on the hill and there were row upon row of perfectly identical flats, masquerading as miniature houses nestled amongst the greenery of newly planted shrubs and evergreens. Of course Tomas lived on the row of flats, the one near the mouth of the official entrance, house number 6.

Fumbling through his jacket pocket I found his house key and opened the door. No one was in except for Buzby, the masquerade toy dog that Tomas had brought from Paris to guard the entrance of the house. Pets were prohibited, but since Buzby was stuffed and quite dead the sanctions did not apply.

First I took Tomas to his room. This was quite an achievement in itself as he was slipping into a semi-comatose state and soon would be rendered catatonic with the effects of the alcohol. Then I plied him with water, never the beverage of choice, especially if there was Cola in the fridge. He began to revive after an hour or so and then started to get amorous. I was not in the mood. Frankly I wanted to slap him for wasting my night. But since unofficially he was "my man" and I was the one who found him, it was my duty to sober him up. Three rounds of 'La Marseilles' later and he was in a half fit condition to talk. I was exhausted. It was close to two am and his flat mates would soon be coming back. Too tired to walk home under the moonlight sky, I slipped into bed, fully dressed, with Tomas. We cuddled under the sheets. This was my first official sleep over. Sleep-sleep let me add.

"You really are a secret sensualist," he whispered to me in the morning after he roughly kissed my forehead with his now moistened lips. Turning slowly to him, I met his face-to-face expression and ran my small fingers through the ridges of his stomach and outlining the muscular indents with the movements of my fingers. All the while I could feel his breathing warm and wet clouds of air and then there was the slow controlled breathing to mask any over representation of excitement. My lips met his; we kissed and touched each other in a way I had not experienced before. He was holding me and it felt great. I wanted more, despite the warning voice telling me to stop before I got into worst trouble.

"I want to fuck you Max."

I jerked back.

I was not ready for this. But all the while he was kissing me and I was responding in a way that I had never done before. Hurriedly I pulled away from him and began to smooth over my crumpled clothes. I was half way out of the door before he caught my hand. Confused, he protested, that he thought I wanted this. I did not know what I wanted. He had aroused feelings within me that I could never have dared imagine ever wanting.

Just the suspended anticipation of it all was driving me crazy. I could only imagine what he would be feeling.

"If you walk out of that door Max," he shouted, "don't ever expect me to take you back."

I kept on walking in the golden sunlight in my crumpled clothes back to bedroom where it was safe, warm and I was still mummy and daddy's little girl.

For months afterwards I contemplated that day's events in the solitary confines of my room, I considered his reaction as penance for my earlier sins of omission. Even now I had a very catholic approach to suffering. Suffering had a necessary part to play in the whole schematic circle of events. It was a learning curve. Something to be undergone, like trial by fire something that turned you into a shining glowing phoenix out of the ashes.

He had sounded deliciously different and yet somewhat familiar. I discovered that this familiarly was the common vein most men share in their attitudes towards sex and how to get it and how they feel towards rejection. I flattered myself that I was a sphinx without a secret. I was unwilling to be unraveled. I did not want him to deconstruct the mystery of my actions that night, to know the riddle of the sphinx. That would have solved the equation between us. I felt that some equations are better left unsolved. For they remain in a constant state of flux and it is this flux that creates the interest and fosters the relationship. Sometimes too much information is damaging. He no longer found me hypnotically fascinating, whatever fascination he had for me had rapidly evaporated like a shallow puddle in the noonday sun. It is the interest in the unknown that generates that hypnotic fascination. Now that he had deconstructed me I now seemed as ordinary, lackluster and common place as everyone else. So not to question would have kept our eternal equation unsolved.

Why did I live the way I did? Because I was a bonafide extremist. I never did things by half measure. Either I sucked all the marrow out of life or I was hermit. There was no balance so to speak. I hated to compromise, and I only ever truly felt my own person when I was on the furthest corner of extremity. That was my natural terrain. I took no prisoners and made no compromises. To live in between these ways would mean to make compromises it would mean to acquiesce to ordinariness.

The supposition is that living an exciting life by doing lots of exciting things makes you an exciting person. This is the first fallacy. It is the converse. An exciting person leads to an interesting life. To suggest that living a life is to live a life is a series of events one has "to do" is to see only part of the picture. To truly suck the marrow out of life one has to do more than merely experience events, as if each experience is a bizarre initiation process culminating in a gold medal of events. One has to live life note all of the subtle nuances that are part of the event, the voice, the sounds the smells all the minutiae that if you fail to stop and blink for a while you would miss.

My new lifestyle was the most rebellious thing I had ever done. It questioned the lifestyle of everyone I knew back home, everyone who was different to what I imagined the norm to be. Boyfriends, smoking, alcohol, partying, and now sex, my lifestyle questioned their relative happiness, my lifestyle suggested that their so-called "value system" had an important element missing. That the essence of happiness and contentment is not the event it is the emotion reigning in. That generating happiness need not be dependent on ensuring a consistently appealing environment. Instead it could be extracted out of the harshest terrain and the most testing surroundings. That happiness is not an event but an emotion.

Already I felt that I had grown as an individual from that experience and that now I had the potential to bring a great deal into a relationship, love, commitment, understanding, humor, warmth, generosity, understanding and intelligence that at the beginning of the academic year I had not been able to do so. I did not want someone to make me happy I wanted someone to heighten whatever happiness I had with me now that I was free. Before I lacked one thing within me, I was still a newly growing person finding out and discovering my opinions, likes and dislikes. Now a pattern had been established. I was my own person with my own established boundaries of tolerance. I was bound to try again. Wasn't I?

The Beautiful People Club

Chapter 5

I emerged from my 'Tomas funk' in a somewhat unexpected manner. I was in a down town club in my usual get up, wrinkled jeans, trainers and a fitted top and less than nothing makeup when I saw Tomas. He was standing this time, but with the support of another well dressed student. Not so beautiful but she projected her allure and he radiated towards her. She was his Israeli Enchantress and she made a fire fly out of him, for there was enchantment in the air that night. He saw me turning his head towards me briefly in a manner that resonated my insignificance towards him.

Dora, giggled as she saw me. I knew then that she knew everything. She was the competition, a competition in which I had already lost the first round of the fight. It was then I formulated my plan. I had been edging towards it for some time. Now it took wings. I was shabby in comparison. I saw my social inadequacies and felt woeful. Deciding on a plan for reinvention, I would change myself to be that type of girl, the desirable type. I wanted to be in control of the situation, to navigate my ship in any waters to be the captain of my social destiny. It was decided then. But I needed help.

Leaving the club, I walked the long walk back to my dormitory with only the moon and stars to keep me company. The breeze in the air contained a chilling scorpion's sting and I hugged myself warm walking first quickly past the promenade and then slowly up the hill. The police were active with their speed guns that night, catching drunken students in clapped out cars.

My brain roared passed tonight's events, focusing on my recovery plan for my now battered and bruised self esteem. It was only a matter of time before I would have formulated a fitting plan for retribution. For I was a revanchist at heart. More than showing Tomas and Dora, I would show the world that I could coldly and calculatingly Svengali myself.

Reaching for the last cigarette in my soft top packet I pulled it out carelessly and threw it towards myself, catching it in my opened mouth. This was a luxury of last resort. My finances had already dried up and now I was approaching bankruptcy. I had no funds left to further the extravagant lifestyle that I dreamed about. I needed a job.

The next morning I walked to the Student's Union hoping for a part-time job. The bar was already half filled with midday stragglers. The bar staff stood languishing behind the bar waiting for the next customer to serve a pint to. Dave, the fifty six year old manager was there it was eleven-thirty and he already had a half finished pint of beer waiting for him on the table. His cheeks and nose were covered with red criss-cross lines over his once handsome face. Staring at me quizzically he asked me what I wanted to speak to him about. This was no time for the language of diplomacy. I blurted out my desperation. Observing my behavior as it to make some kind of mathematical calculation, he nodded to himself thoughtfully, and then gave his response in a slow deliberate manner as if the weight of the world rested on this decision.

His answer was a resounding yes. I was to work behind the bar during the week and also one night a week during the weekend rush, according to the weekly schedule. He shook my hand and then threw a regulation blue tee-shirt to me, containing the Student's Union's logo on it. This was the uniform I would be wearing. Katie turned up moments later. Her shift and my first day was about to begin in ten minutes. A veteran of bar work, she promised to show me how to pull a real pint and all other necessary modus operandi of the job. I had secured finances; I would later secure my style quotient.

Despite the gentle hum of the air conditioning, working behind a bar was hot and hard work. I had worked up a good sweat and my blue tee shirt began to cling to me. Beer and lager stains covered my clothes for this was messy work for even the most proficient barman, and I was a newly inducted novice. The floor was wet with puddles of alcohol of different varieties all mingling like a melting pot on the floor of the bar. We strove to avoid these small ditches as we walked the short walk between customer and the drink they wanted.

I was to watch Katie on many occasions pull the perfect pint, with the requisite amount of head. It was all a trick of the wrist, the way the beer glass was held at an angle to the tap, leaving a dark liquid in the bottom of the glass and half an inch of pale creamy foam on the top. This was the stuff dreams were made of as I wrestled with other bar staff for customers, compliments and the occasional drink. In Dave's eyes this was the best job in the world, the only one where you could drink on the job. Well at least in Dave's bar.

At the end of our shift, after the last malingerers had left, Katie and I strode out laughing and joking, while my feet ached. I had never had a job before other than working for the family in my father's one room accountancy office. This was like nothing I had ever seen. The way the students jostled for attention, screaming out their orders to us and we would respond, Katie as always ready to give a fitting answer to any one who challenged her authority. Me, hesitant, forever doubting my capabilities in this fast paced learning curve that I was undergoing, but loving every minute of the attention I had always craved but never got. These were the halcyon days of peaceful gentle calm. Yet I was soon to be energized by another force which suggested the possibilities and probabilities that life held. Soon I was to stride into another world partly my own making, partly of my desire. Dream carefully for we never know what will, come true.

I walked the short walk alone from the Student's Union back to my dorm against the background of a starlit sky of the darkest, moodiest, indigo and the crescent moon hung in sadness. Kicking imaginary pigeons on the stone tiles I felt I hand grab and then pull me. It was Alex. I could feel his hot breath on my face and his lips against mine. He was so close but did not kiss me. He merely looked into my eyes and communicated silently all that he felt. I felt the pull and thrust of his body against mine we were so close and there was no one about. No danger signals arose from me, some how despite his greater strength and height I felt fully in control that I was the commander of this night time drama.

Finally he spoke, "Curvy women in tight fitting jeans are a god send for me." He said this smilingly as he pressed his lips towards me. I frowned, he spoke again "Well at least one of us has had the opportunity of being sidetracked by lustful images." And he smiled again.

"Oh lucky you!" I retorted for want of saying anything better. I could feel my heart beating and all the usual clichés. Those eyes, how he looked at me…he knew how to use them to masterful effect. Yet still I twisted my wrists from the control of his hands as I sought to remove myself from his grip. I was unable to enjoy the moment, all I felt was my usual fears and trust, well that was an emotional commodity that I had run out of. I wanted it all but on my own terms. I left him stunned on the pavement as I walked away from him.

That night the sun drowned into the sea only to resurface in the morning like a newly born phoenix aglow with fire. As I waxed and waned like the moon, I held my tears in my hands whilst different thoughts echoing from me. Did I hate Dora and Tomas? Of course I did. Hate is an acquired taste, a foreign fruit, in essence it takes time to develop a taste for it. It is an acquired skill, requiring reason, wrath and lots of justification. The Russian Philosopher Bakunin had once said that "the passion for destruction is also a constructive passion." And so it would be for me. I was about to tear down the citadels of myself to resurrect a new me.

Was this dharmic destiny? Duty verses desire and all the things that follow from that realization that our lives are not our own. That in living, we inadvertently live for others, fulfilling their desires and lay the foundations of their dreams and unconscious actions. Be that person, mother, father, husband, boyfriend or lover, our lives are not our own and I was shackled to these ideas in the worst way. I was the realization of this nightmare gone awry, and I did not even know it. All I knew is that I had to fulfill my own destiny to be the perfect daughter, the perfect sister and one day, the perfect wife. These were the pressures of growing up and of awareness. And what I would have given, to be careless and carefree but that was not to be my karmic career path.

Filled with wild unfulfilled unrealized and as yet unexpressed longings for a different world, maybe a better world, where I designated the social order of the day, where I was the make shift master of my own mystery play. How long could we live for others, each generation sacrificing their life for the previous in childlike obedience? Cut the cord a little voice inside me spoke with a gentle roar. Cut this intergenerational bond. Be free, because freedom is the only thing truly worth living for, freedom to act, freedom to think, freedom to express that outlandish idea freely that you never wanted to tell the closest soul to you.

In humble obedience to my ancestors, I shifted forward, forgetting everything fighting everything forcing my life to be the way they wanted it to be. I was tired, and wanted no more of this generational Gaza strip. In the back of my mind, I wanted more, I wanted something else. I wanted to change my mind. The mind I made up for me by my family, by my society and finally my friends.

The Beautiful People Club

Chapter 6

It was a balmy September night when we arrived at the Student's Union where most of the students congregated. There were the usual bouncers waiting outside the student's union. Physically they were packed. Big beefy muscular bodies, an armoury against the attacking hordes of students that marched during the darkening hours of the night flashing their annual student's union cards and dropping their hard won cash in the kitty.

Ed was the host DJ that night. "Turn up, tune in and hangout" the posters advertising the gig had said. Posters that Ed had meticulously plied onto every available blank wall on campus.

It was a club in everything except appearance and it was here that the plans I had for reinvention would materialize. Once again I had turned to Katie for help. In her languidity she gave me pointers on how to improve myself. Yet pretty soon I realized that that her help was not enough. I had to apply the methodology of serious student study onto this latest field of interest to really reap the benefits. Although being a borderline nerd I had always had a vestige of cool shoomool within me, thus saving me from total social annihilation.

There we stood together in defiance of the world, Katie and me. Then Alex walked in alone into the smoke filled bar. There we stood, lines and curves, the two women in his life, silently observing him with combusting emotions. For he was a fast talking, wise cracking, hip swaggering wide boy and we loved him for it. With a drink in hand he turned to smile at us, smiling his hundred thousand watt smile. The whole club saw the line up of pearly whites glistening behind those lips. And in return he saw our faces light up in response to his smile. This was a volley of smiles and stares between the two of us.

Whilst we both wore the requisite little black dress and high heels, the effects were in startlingly contrast to each other. It was the comparison of 'curves' verses 'lines' that Alex had often commented on. Katie was by definition "lines" a hard body all sinew and muscle, angular and taut. I was curves, but of course, soft and smooth with the body of a woman and the face of a child in wide-eyed astonishment. That I was curvaceous he had often noted as his eyes followed the outline of my figure. Unknown to me stood a woman in fury.

All the while the music played on and I was having miniature myocardial infarctions as I noticed all the attention that I was getting in my new outfit. Now I realize that that was the last of the Halcyon days, of relative peaceful gentle calm that were happy and carefree with poetic charm.

The music played on and Katie and I began dancing and tantalizing Alex with an appearance that I now possessed. I love to dance, I had spent years as a child dancing at a small private school, learning rudimentary tap, ballet and jazz. All in all I was never the star pupil, but I did learn to shake a tail feather with aplomb. It is interesting to watch people dance, it's a great equalizer. People perceived to be cool can loose this status on the dance floor and heroes are born just for the way they move. Dancing involves skill and confidence. You can tell a lot about a person from the way that they dance. Most people shuffle along to the beat waving their arms around once in a while, some people gyrate wildly but have a good time anyway. Others and this is mainly men, have no rhythm so refuse to dance at all, they are too egotistical and refuse to look silly in front of their peers. Lastly, there is a rare species of person who dances well. They are graceful and sexual but is it personality or is it skill? I have often wondered.

I watched Monk as he arrived on the dance floor. Now he was dancing to the beat. Gyrating wildly with his Muppet show maneuveres in his sweat soaked tank top and cargo shorts. He was a regular at the union, dancing to Nirvana until the lights went out. He was the living heart of the beat, its human embodiment, its soul. He stood over six feet tall and just as gangly, with post teenage sproutings of a beige coloured beard and moustache under a mop of curly brown hair that was already showing signs of thinning. He was called Monk because that had been his calling, his pre-teen dream to enter a monastery. Those dreams shattered under the new pulsating thud of slash rock, and his new found calling under the banner of grunge with Kurt and Courtney as the new God and Goddess of Rock. He was the singing and dancing embodiment of love in its purest form.

That night I too was there to strut my stuff and how. Sometimes you have got to trick yourself into being happy and that's what I did when I danced. No matter what else is going on in the world when I dance I immediately feel better. That Alex was there and the territorial connection between us had been re-established for that one night and I was happy just to be near him.

Now I realize that both Katie and I were dancing for Alex's attention and time but in altering ways. Katie beckoning him directly with her vixen-like maneuveres and me I playing my usual game of ignoring him by being too cool. Silently, secretly furtively I watched him across the dance floor. I was dumbstruck with doubts. Would he come to me again and would we follow our usual rituals? Mr. Predictable was getting harder to predict.

For now his actions had the anger of wounded pride. Of rejected love and tortured times thinking why I did this to him time and time again. If he had been sensitive to me I would have fallen into his arms the very moment he gazed at me with his wondrous eyes. But it was the very edge of his unexpressed rage that drove a dagger between us. It frightened me, his wildness that was kept on so tight a coil that threatened to uncoil by the very actions that enraged him, my behaviour. If he had ever looked at me with true passion and love I would have been his. For who can resist the calling of true love so neatly wrapped up in such a beautiful package.

At the same time to be the object of his lust thrilled and disgusted me. It felt wonderful to be the subject of such adoration albeit unexpressed. Had he been a kinder calmer sane man would I have loved him the way I did? No. It was sheer animalia within a personality bypassed by his higher intellect or fine emotion that drove him deeper and deeper into the recesses of my mind.

The subtle competition between two women had begun. I was entranced but it was someone else whose attention I caught, dancing the way I had always wanted to in my drunken stupor, careless and carefree. Two blue eyes were staring at me. I was momentarily hypnotised. He did not move to the music and previously I would have decided that he was too good looking to be my type but I was feeling reckless that night. My silent dialogue had begun. It consisted of mournful sighs and stolen glances across the dance floor whilst we moved rhythmically to the relentless beat.

Ed put on a song that we both did not like so Katie and I abandoned the dance floor and headed of to the bar. We were headed of at the pass, by our admirers, Alex and Nick, with a bottle of beer in hand. It was a magnificent pose.

Katie immediately encircled them with her eyes, roaming over them like an eagle wondering deciding where her gaze should finally land before she would pounce. I reclined myself against the wall in silent rapture at the beginnings that these were like a new born child not wondering where to lay my feet but still excited by the new found possibilities that life had to offer. As it was two pairs of feet approached us and we waited to see what would happen.

Nick, for I recognized him from band he sang with was standing in front of me, too beautiful to describe in words with his signature smile and blue-blue eyes. He gazed at me and I had to brace myself for I was already giddy with excitement that one feels when one meets ones heart throb for he could have been the heartthrob of millions.

Slowly he began to talk to me, all the usual niceties were observed while he was watching me in that wicked way of his, for he could be Saint Nick or Old Nick, just like his namesakes.

And Nick fell in love with me as softly as snowflakes and just as melting, as I had changed the karmic destiny of my life by changing my name. Now I had Maximum appeal. For this was our twenty first century faerie tale. I had metamorphosed into Max. After all I had changed my life style just to be with him. And a name is a reflection of a personality and a lifestyle; it expresses what you are, who you are and where you are from. But I wanted to blur that statement so I became anonymous, androgynous Max, in name only, but in reality I was still an Indian Goddess.

My eyes flicked over momentarily while I saw the Katie-Alex machinations. She approached the situation with cat like poise; if she was any animal hidden beneath that veneer of humanity she would be a wild cat, probably a tiger. While he looked like a lion, his mane of golden hair falling carelessly and irresistibly like a golden water fall down his back. For she was attempting to yet again cast a spell around Alex, to hypnotise him with desire for only her, and he appeared to be falling but somehow he seemed to be weary and worn out as if giving in less by desire and more by bad habits. Then his eyes narrowed and the eyelashes dropped slowly in provocative evocative revelry of future known pleasures simultaneously his smile spread across his face. He was ready. Unbeknownst to me, even Alex had kept silent about our social interactions and I remained in constant fear of being found out, as always the frightened one.

You are the magic he crooned while kissing Katie. I was momentarily stunned. Was life without her lackluster, that she was the magic and he was happy just to be with her? And I, Max forever the marionette dancing to Alex's tune, whenever it played? No, he wanted Katie but not for love, not for lust but because he could and it was so easy. So easy to flatter her indirectly and find out what thrilled her, what amused her. With a girl like Katie it was difficult to impress her. She needed flattery, big time but she needed it to be done in an off hand manner, so that it did not even appear to be flattery. Once her ego was satisfied she would open up to you other wise she was like Mount Everest, an insurmountable obstacle.

At that point I wanted to be alone. I could not suppress it, what I had done to belong but failed and now what I would do to be alone, it was a Garbo thing. I wanted to be liked by Alex but to be accepted unconditionally with my faults as well. I am not trying to glorify my failings but I did not want to have to pretend to be perfect just in order to get along with people. I am not perfect. I am a human being but beyond that I wanted to be loved, unconditionally, but I suppose that everybody wants that.

For Alex had never asked me out, but instead had beckoned me with the triumphant twang of his bed strings. Not for reasons of modesty I had rejected him. It was never that, it was arrogance and an innate weakness and ego. I wanted to be the one woman who could resist Alex, it was pure ego in action. He denied me love so I denied him action. It was pure ego, as my ego was bigger than my love for him. I did not want to be tossed aside in the morning. For I knew that once I would succumb to him and express my desires I would never be able to refuse him anything, instead I watched him bed a succession of lukewarm women beginning and ending in Katie, but in my heart, (perhaps it was my desire that) they never inspired him. It had always ended quickly and swiftly and Alex was still there and the tragedy was that I thought that he would always be there.

And I suppose this Nick thing, as he grew to know what I was how I felt but still it was ok with him. I never realized why he tolerated my unspoken eccentricity he never would have had I not fitted into his narrow ideal of perfection. Had he not fallen for my so-called Helen of Troy beauty. And he was like no man I had ever known, not that I had known many. He was everything any woman could ask for, he was a tall handsome intelligent alpha male. And these qualities were an affirmation, I had finally become worthy. I am not exaggerating the effect that he had on people; his radiance drew you to him. Even when a crowd threatened to envelop him, he could cut through it with cat like agility, merely because people paused momentarily just to gaze and see him walk by.

Let me explain, have you ever had a dream, a wish that you have nurtured and cherished? Often I debate whether it is bad to dream or just bad to dream unrealistically. You see before I had ever met Nick I had constructed an imaginary creature, this person who would be everything for me. I had invested a lot in these dreams, all my hopes, fears and desires. I wanted a soul mate, someone whom I could talk to, someone who was there for me, someone who loved me, because I did not love myself enough and did not think that I was worthy. I needed to boost my self esteem and Nick, he was my dream man come true. Growing up with all of these longings and desires, I needed love, attention, adoration but I wanted to be cool, to have the right friends, wear the right clothes all of the shit things, but I did not deserve any of it. So these dreams…they really mattered. These were the measurements of my self worth.

Life was a party and we were the main attraction. The perfect couple, a pretty pair of people. We had it all, Nick and Max the unstoppable founding fathers of the BEAUTIFUL PEOPLE CLUB.

The beautiful people club had no geographical location, it existed merely in everyone's head. It was an egalitarian club cutting through class, race, gender and wealth. Membership was bestowed by birth and VIP membership to the club, determined by Nick, enabled member's social access to our company. We decided who we would associate with and why.

Membership based on appearance. Nick liked people with aesthetic appeal and he justified this by pointing towards a biological imperative towards this form of social interaction. For him it was Darwin's forgotten footnote in the evolutionary argument for natural selection. Are you shocked? Don't be, this is done every day. Why do magazines prefer young, pretty, and slender models? Even babies are preconditioned to gaze lovingly at the beautifuls. So isn't it a biological fact that we prefer the company of nice looking people. Everyone aspires to perfection and Nick also did as well in his own extremist fashion. He believed that it was only possible to associate with people on the same level as you.

When I first heard this argument I was disturbed indeed. Nick was talking about things that deep down I knew and acknowledged but would never say out loud. The reason was plain to see for the world is populated with generally less then perfectly beautiful people. How would the average Joe, ordinary but not ugly, like to hear the rants about a self styled club that they could never join? They would feel like outsiders looking in. I began to wonder, did all attractive people feel like this, did they feel that they were better than everybody else. Was their attractiveness worn like armor shielding them against the world?

Beauty has been defined and redefined over the centuries by poets and painters alike, but now scientists can define it with mathematical precision. The physical manifestation of beauty is one thing and one thing only, "proportion" perfect proportion down to less than a millimeter's error. It is an anomaly, less than one percent of the world's population is truly proportional. It is the exception not the rule. But it is the primary purpose of the gene pool, a biological imperative to favor physical perfection over perceived imperfection and we have all succumbed at one time or another.

We had already established that being beautiful was desirable, but was it better? Surely it must be as every woman who buys a fashion magazine or new lipstick knows that she must maintain herself and believes it is desirable. But when every man and woman competes to acquire something that is given by virtue of birth it is an in built mechanism for failure and self doubts. Creating inter gender tension between man and man, woman and woman, and for every one who resists that irresistible urge there are one thousand who spend every moment and every penny to becoming the best at something they cannot hope to achieve without god's divine grace, to become the best at something transitory. Failure creates jealousy at others success in this biological Russian roulette. This is the highbrow Hitler-ite nightmare that has visited us since Adam and Eve and Samson and Delilah.

The Beautiful People Club

Chapter 7

That is what I liked about him, Alex, his smile and the fact that he made me laugh and smile a lot. His smile marked him out, that hundred thousand watt smile and two rows of gleaming white teeth, a dentist's darling, although he rarely went because he never seemed to need to. His smile made him different; otherwise he would have been just another handsome face and not my official smile catcher.

And thinking about him made me remember that so many people seemed to have forgotten how to be happy as if it was a by product and not a goal in itself. That most people couldn't smile any more, it was simply moody stares and dramatic pauses and the eternal maw-maw, air kiss. Irony is that baby's smile a lot, so what happens in those intermediate years before adulthood that makes us unlearn instinct.

Because no one ever smiled anymore or if they did they never smiled enough. Was the world increasing in unhappiness? I hoped not. According to anecdotal evidence we were less satisfied then ever before and there was so much misery and sadness, but even when there was not much to smile about even when he was in the midst of dramatic pathos he would rock you with his laughter, happiness would explode out of you with mighty gusto. It was powerful stuff. I contemplated all of this as I sat on the blanket of bluebells in the middle of the forgotten forest with my love, Alex.

Of course I never really said any of those things to him, not really, I just thought them and felt them and was happy just to be nearby, just basking in that smile. And I thought for that moment that he was the luckiest man alive and I want to be just like him just for that moment.

He turned to me and talked. How we had a horrible sense of failure that permeated our lives all the way through and yet we had everything. This was our generation, a lost generation, Generation X. We had higher expectations than any other previous generations and a greater sense of collective loss, he mused dramatically.

Whilst the sunshine seeped through the sycamores and a gentle wind toyed with the grass and the leaves on the lawn. He sat down as always with his long legs stretched forwards and his ankles and feet knee deep within the bluebell lawn. Then he spoke on top of the blue-green field with the buds quivering in unison to the sounds of his poetry.

"I cannot send myself so I send my hopes, my dreams and my thoughts to you my metaphysical message in a bottle which travels through space and time to meet you.

I throw it into the air and send it through nameless faceless collection of people who found in my dream a belief that they believed in what I believed and passed on my message to you.

And so my words spread like hurricanes across the ocean and the sea and into every corner of the globe and I asked you to send for me so I could be with you to be held by you forever in your ever loving embrace."

"But you never replied and all I heard was the distant echo of the sound of my own voice. I heard the reflection of my own echo through other people, hear me, help me, be with me, I love you."

Alex was just like Salinger's character, in the book, A Catcher in the Rye, all that he ever wanted to do was to find something that he loved to do and do it. It wasn't about the name, the fame or the glory. I mean it was that too, because who would pass it up if it were helpful to them. But really in the final analysis he would pass it up because all he wanted to do was to find a job that he loved to do and to find his niche. He found where he belonged and his dreams were of the most extreme kind. His dreams were creative and you cannot go to a career guidance councilor to tell you what to do and how to become a rock star.

You have to be found so that is why he sent his message in a bottle and he once told me that if he could cut out the heart of his that made him like he is, then he gladly would have done so because in the final analysis it was too difficult to be like this to feel the way he felt. Who knows, who really knew, no one really, who would have heard his prayer, so he spoke to the wind and so he whispered his dreams and let it carry on the invisible thread of human life that ties us all to one another and that sea- carried my dreams to you he hoped.

"In the final analysis it doesn't really matter, I had no choice and if I could stop being like this I would, but I cannot because it is too difficult to be like this and there is a part of me who wants what everyone else wants and the regular things. And I feel that completely within me. Each fighting for supremacy and one moment one side was winning and the other side was loosing. So I felt this wave of constant turmoil churning within me each trying to destroy each other. Because this is not the lifestyle I choose, it choose me and I struggled against it all my life. Alex told me. I felt worthless and unworthy. So now I like surprises and I choose happiness and now I control the karmic destiny of my life.

"And now I am sending my messages in a metaphorical bottle because I realized that bad things happen to good people and I don't know why – but I have chosen to be happy and that is my message to you."

"Before I would have rather preferred for you to think that I was hard and horrible and strong then for you to realize how easy it is for you to hurt me."

"Because secretly I always felt that I wasn't good. That I didn't deserve any of it and that I didn't have the acceptable face of genius. And I always felt that ~I couldn't make it on my own so I needed to run away."

"And I would rather be a mummy to you with my painted face entombed within myself for five thousand years, then for you to see how easy it is for you to hurt me by the way you acted. Because being sensitive makes you vulnerable so I don't want you to see me."

"Because I had nothing to offer but myself and I always felt that I wasn't quite good enough. And I felt I needing saving from saviours. But not anymore. Because now I am the catcher."

"But who catches the catcher? Let the world create an invisible net and catch me if I fall. Even if I am lost and alone and I have no one the world will conspire to catch me."

And I meditated on this moment for a lifetime and whilst the sands of time whistled by. Whilst armies of angels carried my whispers on the winds.

"And I felt all powerful and all mighty because I directed the moons and stars for you. And I will fly through oceans and continents just to be with you and I would realign the heavenly bodies because I love you."

"And I extrapolated myself into time and space because I wanted you to save me when I could not save myself. And I invested my hopes and dreams and they all became manifestations of the same me."

"And I just want to keep you safe from harms way – of course when I want to and for you who wants to see the skyline erupt across the horizon."

"And all my life I dreamt of you and it was your face projected over the horizon and that face was love. My thoughts were always with you and they flew by your side and entwined themselves around you and remained there. And I was always there…never bodily, but in spirit and you felt my presence when you struggled to be happy."

"And so I threw your whispers in the wind so that another catcher would catch your wishes and make your dreams come true. And I realigned the co-ordinates of the stars for you. I felt that internal cosmic harmony because I was at peace with you. And all the while voices thundered past and the skies opened up, swallowing up the sounds."

"And I tied my invisible thread around you so we were bound together in this life and all our other lives because I just wanted to be with you. I just wanted to hear your thoughts. And that moment when we both believed we both became one."

"The moment we believe we become one and you added to the mystery by believing in it otherwise we all stand alone."

Throughout the years I heard the reflection of his echo repeated through the millions of people I met everyday through the constant stream of human traffic that is life but in the end it was my own reflection coming back to haunt me. And did I recognize the face of genius when I saw it and what did that face of genius look like. Tell me would you recognize that face if you passed it or did it pass you by?

"What do you live for?" I asked Alex in wondrous curiosity. He replied that he lived for his true love and that he could die for his true love.

Replying caustically, I said that that is not true, that nothing and no one is worth dying for. He told me that he did not believe me. "You only say that because you have not found true love."

Love is something that is the heartbeat of life for there is nothing better than love.
Love sustains a beggar on a cold winters day.
Love gives fuel to the fire of a poor man's heart.
Love fills the empty belly of a beggar woman who has just fed her children.
And it is the lack of love that turns princes into paupers.
The rich men into slaves.
For love is something that we all crave.
Something that we all desire.
Making us both the master and the slave to a strange beguiling emotion that we want and cannot satisfy.
For love sustains life, it sustains my life, I've lived my whole life as a lover and that is how I wish to die.
For love is illogical, irrational and yet I find it irresistible.
I've loved my true love, in every aspect, every shadow and every form in every way and shape that she is.

For I was so immersed in thoughts of her that I forgot everything and everyone else. For she is everything to me my entire world and I, and I am nothing without her.

How she made me a slave in ways that you cannot imagine that my whole life hinges on one beautiful moment after another. Yet always caught in desperate fears that this is all an illusion that will end with the light of sunrise in the early morning.

Was it all a beautiful dream? I hoped not.

It was purely oral, you know, Alex verbalizing, that's all. Who could resist such gorgeous words? Only "the She"!

Alex said that even if no one hears my prayer and no one calls me back it was still a wonderful way to spend an afternoon. Because I talked to you and I shared my thoughts and I shared my dreams and you listened to me.

So he told the world but no one understood that he was a smile catcher and so his message was distorted and destroyed so he never received a reply.

The Beautiful People Club

Chapter 8

I had not told anyone, but I felt so sad, that I could not stop crying. I felt betrayed, because whatever I had thought about Nick, and all of those years, all of those good feelings that had carried me and all those good thoughts about the way he was with me. Were not true.

That good impression that I had of him had been totally destroyed in a moment and it could not be brought back. Could I trust my own judgment in people? How many times would he unintentionally hurt me?

So I came back to earth with a bump. The boy I knew was gone, and I did not know this stranger who held me in his arms, as my head lay underneath his chin as we embraced.

So I lived in feverish sickness thinking whether I was merely "unfinished business." Nick spoke. "For I've spoken to you about love till exhaustion, because I cannot think, I cannot eat I cannot sleep you have made me forgetful of everything and every one for these are the mad passionate torments of love eternal unending and how I fly to you on angels wings if only to extract another kiss from you... for I've missed your juicy lips. For there is no heaven or hell without you there is only nothingness – an empty space devoid of any emotion. Before you, I never dared or claimed to be happy least I fail but I could not resist you how you have captivated me beguiled me with your being…is this romantic fiction? No these are our love stories that we will tell to our grand children." And so spoke Nick, the ghost of boyfriends past.

All of his words, did they really mean anything? For it was getting harder and harder to resist, I said to myself. Ah the gorgeous words…Nick's gorgeous words they had disturbed me. Am I now awake when I was in a dreamless sleep? Even when time and tide separates us... (I told myself) I would never forget Nick.

And I began to hate her
I always hated her
But that was after
After I discovered what she was
Who she was

For I chose unwisely, I chose naively I just wanted a safe haven for my thoughts
The final element of revenge is betrayal
Betrayed twice
Because she told him whilst she bedded him
I told my best friend and she told the world
I told the Katie Bitch

Bitch by name

For she was a viper tongued vixen to the end, and how
Her eyebrows were pale blond moon crescents
Looming over her true blue eyes
Her eyes darted quick-slow, slow slow slow quick
Always on top of the moment

Star shaped studs affixed to her earlobes
Twinkling at me
She was a bleach blond floozy
Whose mouth would twitch at the merest mention of someone else's failure?
Her face was impossibly beautiful
A row of teeth, which were crooked
Vanity derived at an early age that she would not wear braces
So only her teeth marred the beauty of her smile

And all I ever saw was her smooth face
And if I had looked closer
I would have seen the delicate twitches and reactions to my comments
But I never did, I never did look
Because I wanted to believe that she was my friend
That we had something in common
And unbeknownst to me we did
We had a common goal

I wanted to believe,
That she had my best intentions at hear

That she would do anything for me
As I would do for her
Foolish eh?
That makes me a fool
Doesn't it?
But tell me is it foolish to believe
Or just foolish to believe unwisely?
Because where do you draw the line between this
distinction

Of course she was the last of the great
bachelorettes, wasn't she?
But of course it was all bullshit
Fabulous bullshit worthy of the tag bullshit
And whilst she spoke her rhetoric I believed it
That we were titans
And we would never do this

I wanted to, I was a fool
She never deceived me
Because I deceived myself
Deceived by Katie and Nick

Whilst she angled herself on that chair
Changing the position of her legs
Wrapping around her knees
And artfully repositioning herself
When it suited her to do so
Toe tappy, so happy
Continually
With my head swiveling

Whilst she found her moment

She was a fucking bitch
Fucking him and all the while pretending
Acting out
This labyrinth maneuveres to keep me deceived

Tapping her nose with her boney finger
In rhythm to the beat within her
Twitching nervously
With her veneer, a patina of calm
Of course I hated her
But I didn't always
Once she was my friend
My best friend in the world.

The Beautiful People Club

Chapter 9

I wanted to see Alex; he was the only person left that I felt that was on my side. I was thrashing around to find some meaning, to get an explanation for all of this, an explanation that wouldn't blow my world apart. I was drunk and unhappy. I knew that it was wrong to go to him and tell him my troubles but I wanted to be near him. Our old banter had disappeared a long time ago and I wanted to pour my heart out to him. To tell him all the things that I wanted to tell him before but I was too frightened to. I honestly believed that if I told him everything he would save me because I could not save myself. I wanted to be with him more and more. The façade that Nick and I had created around us was the stuff of myths and legend. I was sick with unhappiness. I had pangs every time I saw Alex and he was always the same. He always treated both of us the same. He appeared totally untouched by everything. I had already had several drinks in my room, vodka, the usual poison erupting and burning at the back of my throat, traveling down the esophagus like a ball of molten larva spitting from a volcano.

The yellow brick road of my life mapped out before me, because I had always felt striated by life under an increasing burden to re-route. I was caught between the twin horns of destiny and desire, pushed and pulled between two different directions. Alex would have said that destiny was bullshit it was all decision, but I always felt I knew better.

There are two choices, contestant number one. Do you choose A or B? Your life depends on your choice so choose carefully, and think that the smallest action can lead to enormous repercussions and so I imagined my future life with Nick.

But I had never before dared to dream of what life would have been with Alex. And for once I imagined the unimaginable, that life was vivid, a cornucopia of colour a blast before me, but no structure. But I had never really wanted that, because practically had never been my forte.

Yes! Lets just run away together Alex, I thought, lets throw caution to the wind and every cliché. I just wanted to be with you because yours was the face that I could gaze upon for an eternity.

So I walked all the way to Alex's house despite the frequent weather reports telling us to stay in. The weather was evil, dark dank clouds hovered above the night sky and rain fell with a vengeance, because the town was a vampire that night. On the seafront the waves crashed against the promenade as I walked to Alex's house, and I was not even afraid enough to turn back, me who hated the water. Long before I had arrived I was soaking wet, tears were streaming down my face but the tears and the rain mingled into one.

I knocked and Alex opened the door.

"Mmm, curvy women in wet clothes, what a godsend!" He said, in his winning grinning fashion. He welcomed me into the kitchen with his one hundred thousand watt smile. He was cooking dinner, nothing elaborate. This was Alex, the Alex who did not care for food, who ate to live. The pasta was boiling in a large pan and Alex had already fried half an onion and a few pieces of garlic chopped up in a small frying pan. He opened a tin of tomatoes and stabbed the contents of the tin repeatedly with a small knife to chop up the tomatoes. Then he added some mushrooms and the chopped tomatoes to the onions. All the while he was mumbling incoherent happy things. He made me smile, I helped myself to a half empty bottle of beer that was on the kitchen shelf and watched as he serenely walked around the small kitchen stirring each pan whenever he felt that they deserved his attention.

"You look terrible" His statement was true. I was a mess. My hair was slowly drying but my wet clothes clung desperately to my outline in the dimly lit room.

"Do you want to talk?" He started the ball rolling.

I had so many things that I wanted to share with him. To tell him how things really were with Nick. How I wanted desperately to end it but couldn't. How I wanted to wrap myself up in him forever, but all I said was "are you in a rush?"

He smiled sweetly "Yes I am, not in a big hurry but yeah I have a session tonight at the club. I said I'd be the DJ tonight at the Waterfront. I've got to be there for nine. But hey we've got half an hour or so to talk if you still want to."

"Do you want a towel to dry your hair or something?"

"Not a towel, definitely not a towel, but 'something' would be nice. I thought. I'm fine….really. I'll be dry soon anyhow." I replied stiffly.

How do you tell someone that you love them, when you've missed the boat? I had had the opportunity and I blew it…magnificently. I held on to this thought as I had made the eternal trek to his house. On the way I had tossed a coin, it was heads and the decision had been made for me. I told him. "Love you. I've always loved you. Say something Alex."

Raindrops were suspended from my earlobes and I turned to face him, to face his expression and I ran my small fingers through the ridges of his stomach, which outlined the muscular indents of his body with the movements of my hands. All the while I could feel his breathing, warm and wet clouds on my face, slow controlled breathing to mask any representation of excitement.

"Max, I don't love you." Statements and explanations were to follow but there were no admonitions, this is what he said as he held me whilst gently pulling me closer so that I could almost hear his heartbeat.

"You do deserve an explanation. I promise I didn't fake my feelings, but to be honest I have just met someone else and no I don't know how things will work out, but I suspect that it won't go too far. But Max between the two of us the basic difference was always distance, not just geographically but conceptually. Really I don't think that I could ever bear to hear the disappointment in your voice when you realized that I was not what you imagined me to be. I don't want to lie about my intentions to you. I am willing to lie about many things, but this is a bit too much. If we did end up together, I could not bear to hear disappointment in your voice."

Initially I didn't react, but I imploded internally, I was a shell. There was nothing left inside. I blinked back the tears. I didn't want him to see my tears, but for whom was I crying for?

"All this time…I thought you loved me, all these years. I thought we had an unspoken bond. I'm so sorry, I embarrassed you. I was wrong. I'll leave."

I headed to the door and he pulled me back. "At least stay until the rain has stopped."

"It's going to rain all night." I spat out.

"I've got to go to the club soon, but at least stay here and dry off then we'll really talk. There is no one here at the moment but someone will turn up inevitably."

He then proceeded to explain.

I think I always wanted to keep you close, it was selfishness on my part to keep you closer than close, because I loved you Max, I always did. But I could never love you. I know you think that that is a distinction without a difference, but there is a distinction and it is real. How do you tell your best friend that you love them but cannot love them? Max you are my best friend and I love you. But I cannot love you. Because I've tried to keep you close but always maintaining that equilibrium would have been easy had you never said those words that you love me. I felt the push and pull of our equation going awry many times. But that was it, I love you and I love being with you, but I could never love you not the way you wanted me to love you.

And I love being with you but I could never be there for you – the way you wanted me to be. So I just sat and waited for the right one. And your wrong Max, I don't love you. And you're right Max, I do love you and I've always loved you. But not the way you wanted me to do.

And that is the madness of our mathematical equation, is that we are all in love with the wrong people.

And the tragedy is that I'm not in love with anyone else and you cannot prescribe love as if it is necessary medication to be taken at the right time and at the right moment morning noon and night. That's not life that's a jail sentence. And if it had been anyone else I would have done it anyway but you know what? I did love you and because I had feelings for you. I never wanted to wake up to see the disappointment in your eyes when you realized that I could never reciprocate the love that you felt.

It does matter, it matters to you and because it mattered to you it mattered to me and only because it mattered to you. If you had been carefree and careless I would be with you now even though I would care less. But you always cared too much and I couldn't bear to hurt you twice.

I mean where do you draw the line between friends and lovers? The love that friends share and the love between lovers? Because I love you and I always did and I always will but not in that way. You are the person that I care about most in the world and you are beautiful and everything. But if only you had cared less I would be with you now but the weight of your love drove a wall between us only because I knew I could not reciprocate the intensity of your feelings. Yes I had the desire, I always had the desire and yeah it's still there, but not that love.

Does this make any sense? He said.

I nodded dumbly.

Did any of this make any sense for anyone who had ever been in love? I asked myself. He was a bad man, may be even a mad man, but I was the unfortunate one never to realize it. I had wanted him, yearned for him, to possess him, mind body soul to hold him captive for an eternity. And I had felt such sweet passionate torments of desire whenever I looked at him or even dared to touch him. And finally I had even aspired to be what I thought he wanted me to be. He made me quake with desire, so much so, that I could only bear to look at him for a moment or two. Any longer than that I felt as if the whole world, nay the whole universe would have become privy to our unspoken secret. For this was love in all its manifestations.

I slumped back into a large sofa and wrapped up in myself I rocked myself holding my knees close to my chest.

The doorbell rang.

Alex went to the door. Two pairs of footsteps approached. I turned and looked up, and there was Nick. His face was the perfect mask of rage. Quietly he asked me where I had been. I told him that I had been here for a short time but had been wandering aimlessly in the rain.

"You had me so worried. What the hell do you think you were doing? I have been everywhere to everyone. Come on let's go home, I am so tired."

I smiled a brittle broken-dreams smile. Turning to Alex I said "Goodbye" I kissed him on the cheek. "Thanks for looking after me." I said as I squeezed his hand gently.

"Anytime." He said momentarily confused, then finally comprehending.

I walked out of the house, behind Nick, who was scolding me as if I was a lost and lonely child waiting to be found. I had to escape so I squirmed under the grip he had on my shoulder.

"Wait Max, don't go just yet." Nick ran behind me, his long strides soon caught up to me whilst I ran to the promenade and lent over the metal bars.

The waters were deadly, wave after wave crashed on to the road as we were ducking to avoid the torrential rain that was hitting us from all sides, my clothes already sodden and my soul depressed followed by Nick who was following close by trying to make sense out of all of this.

A huge wave engulfed me and I was dragged into the water. The riptides were deep dangerous and deadly that night. Even a strong swimmer would have drowned, and I could barely swim.

Those minutes felt like eternity upon eternity tied together by a loop of string. Do you know what I felt that moment as I was submerged in the icy cold waters, my body bobbing up and down with the waves carrying me back and forth? I felt fear in all its manifestations.

What is fear to you? Do you know, do you really know what it is? If not I will tell you.

Fear is the slow steps behind you on a dark night as you walk back home alone.

It is a synaptic twitching in your brain.

It is predicting the unpredictable, trying to scrutinize all of the possible outcomes and then failing.

Fear is being terrorized by an unknown ghoul, a ghoul who haunts your days and nights.

It's a thought analysed obsessively.

It's your worst nightmare that MAY come true. Something that paralyses your body into inaction, whilst inside your mind you are screaming, screaming for release. "Let me out of hell!" you cry – it is a construction of your mind's worst fear.

What is your worst fear?

Fear is not that which comes true, it has no material form.

A manifestation can be fought and overcome if you are brave. Fear is a manifestation in suspension.

Suspended absolutely – a hinterland's of your mind's construction.

It's the halfway house between the idea and its material fact. The dreaded ghoul that threatens to appear but never does…in a way that you can fight it.

So succumb to the terror.

Fear is breathing deeply for air, nay gulping faster and faster and still you suffocate.

Fear is the unknown, it is a phantom in your mind that infests every muscle and thought and deed. It controls your movement, it permeates your life as you try to counteract it, as you try to think logically but you cannot. It is overpowering and overwhelming

Fear is never violence, it is the threat of violence. Violence is a material manifestation, the logical conclusion, something that can be fought and overcome – if you are brave. Fear is more insidious it cannot be fought externally. It is an ongoing internal battle with yourself, you verses your senses.

Recognise your weaknesses.
Acknowledge them.
That you are afraid – but you don't want to die.

Fear is retribution without reason.

Fear is inertia – an inability to do anything. Paralysis of the body, whilst the mind overheats and churns with worries that are all consuming…that my friend is the nature of fear.

Fear is a subtle hint, a whisper in the breeze that grows.

Fear is a mind fermenting poisonous thoughts and hatching plans that fail.

Fear is the very opposite of love. Hate and love are "two sides of the same coin." Hate and love are reactions but fear has no action.

Fear is paranoia.

Yes, I was afraid, afraid for my life.

Fear is being afraid and having no one to talk to, no one to tell.

Fear is loneliness in a crowd, crying out "save me" but what is there to fear? The lights are bright, people are all around and are laughing and enjoying themselves, but your heart has been gripped by an invisible glove wringing out the very life force from you. No one hears your muffled cries...you might as well be alone.

Fear is having a terrible story to tell that no one wants to listen to. So how can you speak?

Fear is transparent daemons.

Fear is feeling worthless and unworthy.
You have no one.
You are no one.
You – are – all alone.

Fear is a mental trap, it's all in the mind and you are the architect drawing out diabolical plans, setting the parameters and constructing that jail. But you don't control your destiny or the outcome...so you believe...so you fear.

Fear is being caught on a crescendo, a wave that drags you deeper and deeper until you are pulled down to the murky depths.

Fear is your heart beating to a rhythmic beat, a tribal beat, pounding faster, harder, quicker, louder, it is more and more and more.

Fear is being hunted and haunted.

That's what I felt that long night as I ducked and dived in the waves that pulled me in and pushed me out.

Fear is the un-definable, that which defines definition.

Fear is acquiescing gracefully because you have no choice.

Fear is a zealot like belief in the omnipotence and omnipresence of daemons.

Fear is being afraid and having no one to turn to – no one to talk to as you howl silently at the moon.

Fear is amnesia that anything good has happened to you, ever happens to you...or will happen to you.

I was afraid of the dark, afraid of the rain, afraid of the torrents flooding my lungs as I pushed and pulled for air. The currents pulled me down but the waves pushed me up.

Make no mistake, there is no escape.

For who can escape the torments of their minds – their thoughts

Only death is the final escape.

A quickening and then a pause – hasn't life oozed out of you yet?
But aren't you dead already? You wish for it, you crave for it, to take you into its cold clammy winged embrace. You are no more, you rest in peace.

That was it. I feared no more.

The Beautiful People Club

Chapter 10

Small bird-like features of extravagant delicacy, his hair cut to an almost close crop, his sharp beak-like nose and the quick tilt of the head from left to right, small mouth movements. His was a hawk-like gaze with a sudden narrowing of the eyes. And there remained a certain languidity in his stroll which was synchronized to disguise the nervousness that weaker animals possess. Nick was that bird of camouflage, with his rapid eye movements when suddenly sighted and sought out.

Nick was a bird-man not a second to Charlie Parker, Jazz musician trumpeter and saxophone player extraordinaire, but a man-bird for all the bird mannerisms he possessed.

Bird man did you ever want to flap, flap, flap your wings and fly away when you felt afraid as you strut, strut, strutted yourself around me? Peacock in everything including appearance. His bird-like movements on his handsome face. Nick played it so safe for so long that he practically slept his life away. Where were all the risks he never took? All of the adventures that he had never had, all the dreams that he had only dreamt. He lived his life in a coma. His was a one-talent wonder because he cruised on one- ability for most of his life. No in fact a two talent wonder because it takes talent to survive for so long and so secretively as such. Even as you cocked your head and crowed about your one achievement?

No one knew your secret Nick, do they? They don't know what you did that night. They know what you did that day, how you plotted his life away.

Nick, Nick, Nick.
How you let his hand slip.
When you threw your arm for me.
You let him drown deliberately.

Where you ever afraid?
As you plunged his face in the waters.
Alex was at the end of the chain.
Neck deep in water.

And so he drowned that night.
In the waters blue.
There are only three left now.
Me, Katie and you.

It's your one achievement that you live the way that you do and no one knows like Alex knows. Like I almost knew.

Because that night was different, the town was different. The town was a vampire that night. It slashed his wrist and took the infusion, not of blood, but of liquid life, Alex's life. And it was greedy, it greedily gobbled up its victim that night and burped out the whole when finished. It fed on life whilst they watched it grow, watched the waves grow while it threatened to engulf the crowds standing on the perimeters.

Of course that wasn't the real tragedy. Death was only incidental. Ironic really. The real tragedy lay in the fact that no one cared. No one did anything. People paused, the crowd huddled together to watch the sight. Rather like the guillotine executions during Robespierre's reign of terror. Old ladies hunched together underneath the guillotine knitting away, there for the entertainment, whilst counting bloodied heads into baskets one, two, three, four.

This was a real life drama unfolding in front of their very eyes. All that was needed was one person, just one more person to make that human chain longer. Just one more, one more pair of hands.

With devastated irony I knew…of course I knew, but I didn't have empirical evidence for Nick was a virtuoso of deceitful criminality. For as Nick told me many times it is so easy to miss what is in front of your face, but you catch a whisper, everyone listens out for that. So I internalized my feelings, I contained it, when trying to comprehend the terrible rhythm of life and finally death. Whilst all the while, I silently imploded. And the wind whistled through the trees – the verdant leaves rustled with fury.

The Beautiful People Club

Chapter 11

It was my immortal spirit that held onto me from the inside, watching me, holding me, protecting me, keeping me alive, inhaling through me, laughing whilst I laughed, wiping my tears. So you see I never really felt alone and whilst I slowly died, it watched over me, hovering above my body whilst I waited to die, whilst life almost left me, captured in that iota moment of space and time.

My immortal soul met other souls also caught in the same microsecond, souls that streamed past, souls that screamed past – lost souls, laughing souls, exhibiting that same emotion that they felt whilst they almost died, but no one, not a soul at peace.

Because we were all caught in that layer of space and time, our times were different and our reactions were different. There was no warmth or cold around, just nothingness, in that eternity microsecond whilst my head sloped on my shoulder and ventured into past chartered territories.

And that micro-moment eclipsed all other, that moment whilst I almost died and death was one option and life was the other. But I was caught on the twin horns of a life-death dilemma and I was afraid to die, I was always afraid. To cross the barrier, but life now held a nothingness for me, not quite leaving, not quite going.

You see souls are enormous things, enveloping and folding into every crevice, surrounding and submerging you in their immortality.

My eternal immortal soul that loved me and almost left me alone in waters deep.

Whilst my lungs flooded with waters, and my soul emerged soaked, my everlasting, ever loving soul that almost left me.

In those microsecond moments I dreamt of all the dreams that I merely dreamt, and I wanted to believe in the possibility of everything. But I had set limits on myself and I had limited my opportunities and I had created artificial barriers. That I had not accounted for every second of my life and when every second is precious, and I became jealous of every moment of my life that had rolled by unnoticed in what now seemed like a life long lethargy.

As they pulled me out of the water I remember thinking that I was not quite myself that day. All that I could think of at that moment was that I was feeling rather deaf or that I couldn't decode the sounds in order to adjust to that murderous pitch or frequency of the noises. Yes that was it and yeah I'll have to talk to someone about that. I wanted to ask permission. Can you believe that? Can you really believe that? Is it really alright for me to lie down? I think I fainted. How quintessentially English is that?

I felt a perfect peace, but doesn't everyone say that? Totally mute and I suppose that is what happened when the brain overloads and there has to be a short circuit somehow, somewhere and so it was with me.

That night the sun had also drowned into the sea only to resurface in the morning like a newly born phoenix aglow with fire. I woke up in a hospital that was clinically clean. With the sunlight flooding the large Victorian windows and a light breeze entering. Many pairs of unfamiliar eyes peered into my waxy face, felt my pulse. Calm and soothing voices asked how I was and was everything ok? Did I know everyone was worrying? But now everything was ok. I was ok and there was no danger. It seemed as if blurry blobs with different coloured halos or snowmen outfits surrounded me. They hovered two foot above my face buzzing noises too and fro above me and too me. Some times these blobs buzzed at me but I was deaf somewhat (in one ear at the time). It sounded like a familiar chattering from afar though I couldn't decode it. I merely sat up within myself aware that the blobs were flying back and forth and in and out.

Occasionally, I nodded sagely and sometimes they spoke English in muffled soft voices. "Are you alright? They would ask. Followed by "Hmm, yess…" And I nodded sagely as my eyes blinked behind the luminescent brilliant white of the lights and the walls.

The Beautiful People Club

Chapter 12

There are so many unhappy people in the world and I was just one of them. Was there anything I did not all ready know or had analysed over a million times over in my head? I became envious of everything and everyone. I felt as if I was fighting against invisible odds for mine was a bi-polar reaction of love and hate, I loved him and I hated him, who him? Who else but Alex? It is hard to express your love to someone and find that they do not love you, especially when has fate conspired to steal what ever opportunities of revanchist behaviour you may have against them. The same thought tortured me, that aging is natural, it is a sign of decay and conversely it is a sign of life because only lifeless things do not age. For Alex had achieved immortality in my minds eye he would forever be beautiful. Like Samson the length of his hair signified the strength of his beauty, even as I become an old woman with knarled hands and grey hairs day by day.

Now that he was gone and I had seen a million people pass by it was his head that I saw on everyone. I saw his face everywhere. His was the face that greeted me where ever I went, on every poster, TV screen, every passenger, every pedestrian and always looking at me with those terrible eyes, that thirst for knowledge, always questioning me and all I wanted to do was to catch the outline of his lips on my mouth and feel his burning presence next to me once more. It was all that I could do, for I desired him, as I was drowning in a sea of my own desires. Whilst all the while that distant echo drove deeper and deeper and deeper within me.

Was this the sound of madness tinkering through the rooftops of my mind? I asked myself. For I had become infused with the fury of my own rhetoric.

But enough of my melancholia. Adventure, I was still up for it, so I left…in a Holly Golightly fashion. I flipped, I fled, I flew anyway from that town and to a city, that city, the city of cities. New York. I had always liked the idea that if I needed to I could and would be able to just throw everything into a suitcase and leave. Smiling dangerously without my eyes only with the corners around my mouth, for this was the first feelings of freedom, to just drop everything and everyone superfluous and just go. As if there was romance to the escape.

I liked to sit back and watch people in the airport lounges, different hairstyles, races, classes meet and mingle and diverge at the epicentre of travel. The smarts the scruffies the well traveled (seasoned travelers) the stylish and the squashed waiting around for a lift or for someone to collect them. There were brassy blond women with turkey necked double chinned flapping in double Dutch (or so it seemed) whilst talking, presumably about todays gossip. The chattering classes!

All the while I heard the distant drove of the turbines in the foreground as we passengers waited to board the airplane and the buzzy hum continued around us. We were surrounded by the rumble of passing aircraft and human traffic on the airwaves.

Patchwork quilt of yellow phosphorous lights as the plane glided on the tarmac. The lights were spread out across the city, these lines of demarcation had already been drawn and though the land was dark and a layer of billowing cloud lay between yellow lights like row upon row of denim rivets. I could see them kriss-crossed across the city from far above. We left this wet and windy city only after a delay because planes cannot land in high wind speeds so we waited. In all of this drunkenness the airhostesses brought on miniatures and soft drinks and plastics, napkins, pretzels prewrapped to perfection.

And the engines roared for take off and the engine wings revolved and I felt that turbulence on the tarmac as we made our ascent onto the skies. The lights looked like the Nile Basin from far above. Far away, higher and higher and higher the golden yellow lights blurred into a golden haze although distant lights could be seen.

The weather was non descript that day, not too cold, a little windy, grey skies and grey clouds surrounding the plane, it was a typical English day.

Descent was smooth apart from the occasional juddering as the plane climbed from the skies to meet the earth underneath. And underneath the world revolved at right angles and it seemed as if I could even see the curvature of the globe underneath us, spinning at its maddening speed. And there was the haze, always the haze, where light and fog mingled into one to produce a hazy golden glow.

Every once in a while the wings dipped down and we circled the landing rather like an eagle or a falcon circles its prey from high up in the sky. Occasionally I saw the beep beep beep of a passing white light of another plane and there was a red light between the two white ones. The red light served as a warning perhaps red equals danger? To keep a safe distance because there is a plane approaching and not a flying torch or a learner witch on a broomstick.

The lights mangled into one underneath the haze of fog or its more romantic vision. Transparent, translucent swirling mist arose from beneath the city and the plane drove into the mist dividing it and the mist swam in the sky like a reluctant spectre swirling above the city.

Above Manchester the yellow lights were uniform and there were no really notable landmarks crowding the horizon. And that reluctant spectre hovered, mingled, broke of repeatedly forming and reforming into shapeshifting masses of gas way up above the copper coloured lights. Underneath the serpentine curves of the Manchester's river stretched out across the city. Mist arose to form billowing clouds about that lazily drifted by in their cotton wool cloud apparition form. As we arose there were fewer large monuments visible from the sky, even the large sky scrapers were dwarfed from this height and the cars provided twinkles of light like well organized fire flies meandering obediently backwards and forwards on the M62.

I was zig-zagging across the turquoise blue horizons in a transatlantic fury. Then the plane rode beneath us as we descended in a downward motion. We declined in hiccups under currents of air in wave like motions. I felt giddy as the plane flew down to car parks buildings highways. It was a downward slide, we hit the floor running but not in a smooth descent, and the bodies of the passengers were jerked forward. Overhead voices on the tanoy told us to collect hand luggage and wait until it was safe to stand up. Oh and have a safe journey they told us.

I could not wait to make my second escape.

The landscape was breathtaking, and I wanted to jump into the picture, as I imagined a different world, not subdivided between tangible living and the intangible world of death but a different world with a different dimension.

Burnt amber – glowing amber layered sunsets merged into one. Over a black-blue silhouette skyline. There were one hundred or one thousand or one hundred thousand points of reference.

I always felt a small private rush whilst walking into the city, which I secretly felt put its arms around me. The city of Gothomites, for this was the city of the Goths. There were many sunrises and sunsets in New York in that corner of the country, but all I knew that it was blessed with the longitudinal and latitudinal advantage to capture light at advantageous positions and with dramatically different ways and colours.

Back home in Manchester we mainly caught the great grey gloom in all of its manifest hues, from off white to dark pewter, with the odd sprinkling of days coloured by the great bright blue. But those were the exceptional days of summer that I remembered so well.

New York was a city of skies, populated by Gothomites, as proud inhabitants as any other modern tribe that walked the city day and night. And dreams blew like gold dust across the brick streets and the wide boulevards of downtown New York. For the Goths were born to a city, a city of dreams, where dreams were manufactured and anybody had the potential to participate. Knowing this and feeling like this people flooded to these dream makers on Broadway. For nothing ever felt implausible or impossible. Everything was a do-able option. Dreams were there for the taking and there were bucketful's of them lining the streets. Where the celluloid screen seemed more alive than life – this is where illusion ruled and became a second reality more potent than the first because it was fueled by desire. The realisable reality that you could be someone, somewhere somehow if only you knew how. That was the myth but it was also the reality for the lucky few. And I was infected with this madness!

The Beautiful People Club

Chapter 13

"I know that you would like to see a physical manifestation of my apology and here it is and I know how fond you are of inscriptions," Said Alex on the letter "so here are these hieroglyphics that I wrote for you, hoping beyond hope that one day I would be able to give this letter to you, for here you are, a woman of such loveliness that the merest thought that you may never be mine makes me ache" What could I do other than open the letter.

"To my moon-faced Aphrodite,

This is my last ditch attempt at true love. I am just writing what I write and I hope that it all fits into place. Please hear me out for I have reached into myself and seen the truth as if it were some sort of shining orbital.

I am not a spiritual man, I am not a religious man, but in the way that I live my life I have tried to be a good man, I have failed, God knows I have failed. I don't want to harm anyone because I felt that hurt inflicted on my own soul when I harmed you, when I did wrong to you. For me that is the essence of religion, not to do harm, and not the rites and rituals that have separated me from you.

As you know I have never given a damn about anything or anyone that was not me. Mostly I detested those hypocritical people that judged others with standards they did not possess, who were unwilling and unable to live life as they wished that were frustrated but derived pleasure in the miseries of other people's lives, but shielded from view any such tear in the fabric of their own. Now I find myself in the same conundrum."

"They tell lies, the sweetest of poisons to hide their weaknesses. They enjoy seeing other people upset and resent the few moments of happiness that we all wait a lifetime to possess. Such people are the enemies of happiness. They are jealous of love because they have neither the courage nor passion to truly live and suck the marrow out of life. Now I have had the realization that I am the same hypocrite."

I did not regret any decision that I had made but I have endured eternities of pain for it and have had few drops of happiness in the ocean of my life for my sins. I have suffered but at the same time I have felt love. And I can endure it all if I have you for just one moment in my arms so that I may plant a kiss on your forget full lips."

Isn't it the greatest of truisms that the greatest of joys can be mingled with sadness? I only realized how much you meant to me as you were walking away from me with Nick. But even that sadness had a sweetness to be savoured because it brought me closer to you. Frankly I have only contempt for myself, but before you judge me for my harsh words see what weaknesses you possess.

I used to feel that friendship and love were the greatest of feelings after all everybody wants to be accepted for what they truly are only then you can say that you have been loved unconditionally. But now I realize that love, TRUE LOVE is much greater than that. And I do, really I do I swear it, I love you with all my heart without you there is only nothingness. For me your love is an eternal tide as you take all the joy from my life as your footsteps part from me and you bring back all the happiness's flowing back as you draw close to me.

I like most people have lived my life in fear, the very fear of being found out. To have the mask ripped out from under my chin, to be rejected for the flaws that I possess. Flaws that make me feel unworthy of ever receiving love. Even to accept love, you need to be like a plant in a porous pot absorbing all the waters around you. You need to have a certain baseline of humility that is why the proud can never accept love for they are like the door that is bolted with 7 strong locks and chains to guarding an empty building.

Reality is that everyone wants unconditional love, but no one is willing to love unconditionally. This is the source of my unhappiness. This is the broken glass that I have walked on barefooted and bleeding with a fake smile on my face, convincing the world of my virtue. Virtue is there but so is vice. These are the twin horns of my human conundrum. I hate that very hypocrisy that has condemned me to a deathless life. I no longer want to be that hypocrite; frankly I hate this human condition of mine that has made me a wretched slave to the tyrannical whims of others, namely you. I tried to free myself from all of that by simply saying that I did not give a damn that I wanted to be free from all of those ties that bind me to you. I wanted to be free of the jealousies and passions that consumed me so deeply and for so long, for this condition I hold you responsible, you are my jailor, my lover, my tyrant and my friend all rolled into one.

Beauty, truth and loyalty, for me this is the ideal; everything and everyone else can go to the dogs. Now I will endure heaven and hell just living what I believe.

All my life I chose to be unhappy, but when you chose me, I decided to change the karmic destiny of my life, that destiny is all bullshit, its all decision. Because with you by my side, not so secretly I felt that I deserve to be happy and that it is not alright to be unhappy. For I've loved you breathlessly."

All my love,

Alex.

I had so many thoughts and feelings but I still lacked the courage to express them. For words are dangerous things, rather like wild animals. You have to pick your words with care. If these animals escape out of you without any thought then be aware that they may rebound back to you with the same haphazardous force of an uncontrollable juggernaut, spitting out from the mouth of your victim for words always come back to their creator. I should have been dumbstruck with doubt, but I was not, the same thought meandered back to me, why do I love you? Despite initial appearances to the contrary he had no words to soothe, only a fiery love to express. Is this the way that life should be? I asked myself. And I am not saying that it was right I am just saying that that is the way that it was. Once again I was excited by the possibilities that life had to offer. I mused to myself whimsically was love an act or an emotion, love the act or love the emotion. Love the act I had shared with Nick but love the emotion is what I felt for Alex.

On reading the letter I had barely dared to feel and think and love wholeheartedly. I had waited my whole life until Alex could be mine and I could be his I was ready now to love and to be loved and now I had reciprocity.

"I've missed you something fierce," he wrote. "There were so many times that I was so sick and desperate with desire to see you that I did not know what to do" said Alex in his letter. "It was only when I saw you with Nick did I realize how I really felt about you that you were capable of love and how. Thoughts of you made me ache all summer long whilst I plotted and planned my comeback, away from our twisted, tormented reality that had become our lives, I merely required reciprocity and a realization that I wanted a new life with you in it. You incorporate everything I ever wanted my best friend that I loved too little too late. Only to discover that yours is the face that I wanted to wake up to every morning for a lifetime. That my love for you was eternal, unending."

And the world was filled with words again – wondrous words with great meaning and pictures and lights.

Those moments upon moments when I wanted to feel that invisible illusion of his warm caress and I loved that he loved me that he held me and hugged me in his embrace. I felt his skin warm and soft gazing within his face tracing the outline with my fingertips.

I loved it that he loved me because I'd just love to love you for a lifetime and I had always hoped that Alex was for me and that I was for him. All those times that I'd thought that he would be there forever so I had waited. I love you, I love you, I love you, how long I had wanted to hear those words from him.

I had treasured those solitary moments that I had spent alone with him. Remembering the fragrant feeling of his touch and the desire of his warm wet kisses. All of this was done and much more in a quiet corner of the garden. All the while my eyes stored a wealth of information and my lashes shaded my eyes from the glare of his attention and all the while I imagined kissing his face.

The End

The Beautiful People Club

Epilogue

Relationships are delicate things, for they are the physical embodiment of love, in its material form. They can be destroyed with a momentarily lapse or absence of love, but to create them takes a lifetime of love of attentive care so take care over your love to nurture and nature it and let it grow old like an oak and watch it bloom. For in our own way we are all gardeners tending our saplings breathing life into our love and watching them grow with every breath.